Emile de Laveleye, Alfred William Pollard

The Elements of Political Economy

Emile de Laveleye, Alfred William Pollard

The Elements of Political Economy

ISBN/EAN: 9783337077242

Printed in Europe, USA, Canada, Australia, Japan

Cover: Foto ©Suzi / pixelio.de

More available books at **www.hansebooks.com**

THE

ELEMENTS OF POLITICAL ECONOMY.

THE

ELEMENTS

OF

POLITICAL ECONOMY

BY

ÉMILE DE LAVELEYE

TRANSLATED BY

ALFRED W. POLLARD, B.A.

ST. JOHN'S COLLEGE, OXFORD

WITH AN INTRODUCTION AND SUPPLEMENTARY CHAPTER BY

F. W. TAUSSIG

INSTRUCTOR IN POLITICAL ECONOMY, HARVARD COLLEGE

NEW YORK

G. P. PUTNAM'S SONS

27 AND 29 WEST 23D STREET

1884

AUTHOR'S PREFACE.

In this elementary treatise, designed as a manual of instruction, I deviate from time to time from the course commonly followed, because, in my view, the object of Political Economy is not that ordinarily indicated. What is of importance, as it seems to me, is the conduct of individuals and of states, with regard to the production and employment of wealth—that is to say, the moral and political side of our science. In manuals where everything has to be condensed into a few pages, writers often confine themselves to the definitions and to the brief summary of a few general laws. Reduced to this, political economy presents little that is useful.

I have endeavoured to connect my subject closely with those of the other branches of study dealing with human life; that is to say, with philosophy, moral science, the traditions of the past, history and geography. Geography describes the positions of nations, and history relates their annals. No advantage can be gained from the lessons which either offers without the aid of political economy. At the present day it is allowed that the most important part of history is that which traces the progress of humanity in comfort and liberty. To understand this advance from prehistoric barbarism to the prodigious development of wealth which marks our own epoch, a knowledge of economy is indispensable.

In order to show more clearly the close connection which exists between history and political economy, I have not hesitated to multiply quotations from established writers. To the enunciation of each principle I have added an example, a fact, a maxim, hoping that the volume thus enlarged might yet seem all the shorter, through the attention being better sustained.

Some chapters, such as those which deal with socialism, with credit, with commercial crises or with population, will seem perhaps to treat the questions in greater detail than is needed in an elementary treatise. It should not, however, be forgotten that nowadays the young man, on leaving his school or college, finds himself at once beset with these important problems. The social question is the subject of every day discussion ; as to credit, we all resort to it; crises threaten our property at every instant. The question of population is that on which the future of our country depends.

As citizens of a free country we need the training of men. From our earliest years the state claims our attention ; even in childhood political economy ought to make us see that freedom leads nations to prosperity, while despotism leads them to decay.

Need more be urged to prove the necessity of spreading economic knowledge ? The greater part of the evils from which societies suffer spring from their ignorance of this subject. National rivalries, restrictions on trade, wars of tariffs, improvidence of the labouring classes, antagonism between workmen and employers, over-speculation, ill-directed charity, excessive and ill-assessed taxes, unproductive expenditure on the part of nations or towns—are all so many causes of misery springing from economic errors.

Natural science, which is so highly esteemed at the present day, shows man, like other animate beings, subservient to his individual interest. While maintaining that man, a free moral agent, may and ought to listen to the voice of duty, and sacrifice himself for his family, for his country and for mankind, one must recognise the fact that the habitual motive of his actions is the pursuit of what is useful to him. If this be so, is not the science indispensable which shows in what utility consists, and how men united in society may best attain it?

TRANSLATOR'S PREFACE.

THIS translation of M. de Laveleye's *Les Éléments de l'Économie Politique* was undertaken in the hope that the work in its English dress might be useful to students as a supplement to some of the many handbooks already in existence. In English treatises political economy still retains its character of the "dismal science." In *Les Éléments* the subject seemed humanised by a more liberal and broader treatment, and this is the reason of the present translation being offered to the reader.

As the difference in tone is thus the distinctive feature of M. de Laveleye's work, the fewest possible alterations have been made in this edition. A few quotations have been omitted, and here and there an English illustration substituted for a French one. It may be added that the whole of the translation has had the benefit of the author's revision.

Before the present translator began his task a few chapters of Book I. had been already Englished by Mr. G. L. Marriott, the author of the able version of M. de Laveleye's work on *Primitive Property.* The translator desires to acknowledge Mr. Marriott's kindness in handing him over his translation of these chapters when prevented by other engagements from continuing his version.

INTRODUCTORY NOTE.

No APOLOGY is needed for introducing to American readers the work of so distinguished an author as Professor Laveleye. A large number of publications, covering a remarkably wide range of subjects, have made his name familiar to the reading public of civilized countries. Professor Laveleye has been an active literary worker for forty years; and in the course of his career he has thrown light on some of the most important problems of literature, history, and social science. In the field of literature, he published, in his early years, an interesting book on the language and literature of Provence; and has written translations of the Nibelungen-lied and the Edda. In history, he has published a volume on the Frankish Kings, and has made a number of contributions to the recent history of Germany, with especial reference to the events of 1866. Chiefly historical,

but with an important bearing on social and economic
questions, is the well-known work on Primitive
Property, which has been translated into English, and
has done more, perhaps, than any other single work,
to extend the reputation of its author. But it is in
the field of social and economic science that his contributions to knowledge have been of most importance.
He has published numerous books and articles on the
forms of government in modern societies, on the relations of church and state, on several branches of
international law, on education, on economic topics,
and on the political questions of his own country and
of foreign countries. Many of his publications appeared first in the columns of periodicals, notably in
the *Revue de Deux Mondes*, to which he has been for
many years an active contributor. In recent years he
has also made contributions to English periodicals.
The ease and grace of his style, and the clearness of
his exposition, have brought his writings before a large
circle of readers; and their general soundness and
impartiality have made them of great weight with
competent judges. Professor Laveleye was born in
1822, and has been since 1864 professor of political
economy at the University of Liege.

On political economy the more important works of
Professor Laveleye have been : an essay on the Rural
Economy of Belgium (1863), and a similar essay on
the Rural Economy of Holland (1864) ; the Money
Market during the last fifty years (1865) ; the volume
on Primitive Property, already referred to (1874) ;
Contemporary Socialism (1881) ; and the present
Elements of Political Economy, published in French
in 1882. A large number of articles in reviews and
periodicals, many of them of permanent importance,
have also appeared from his pen. Professor Laveleye's
economic views are in strong sympathy with those who
declare themselves to have broken loose from what
may be called the classic system, as built up in the
works of Adam Smith, Malthus, Ricardo, and the
younger Mill. At the same time, he by no means goes
as far as those writers, chiefly German, who declare
that the classic system is entirely superseded. His
position is rather that of the more moderate German writers who protest against the hard and fast
lines of Ricardo's system, and especially against
the dogmatic exposition of Ricardo's system which
has been common with some of his followers ; but
who nevertheless retain, with more or less quali-

fication and explanation, the essential doctrines of the
great English thinker. In the presentation of economic principles by these writers, the qualifications
and explanations, which are undoubtedly necessary to
the correct statement of the principles, sometimes
overshadow the latter, and detract from their incisive-
ness. This fault may perhaps be found with the
present work. The edge may be said to be taken off
the great principles by the qualifications and excep-
tions with which they are stated. But surely this
method of presenting the subject is preferable to the
bald, unqualified, and scientifically inexact statements
which are common in many English elementary books.
And, after all, the divergence of this moderate school
from the classic system is more in spirit than in substance. The spirit of the classic writers was, for
instance, strongly against government interference
in industry. Professor Laveleye, like most German
writers, and unlike most French writers, is not a
decided adherent of the *laissez faire* principle.
Especially in the relations of the state to the working
classes, he has been willing to disregard that principle ;
and his keen sympathy with these classes has sometimes perhaps carried him too far in his views of the

duty of the state, and of the possible results to be
achieved by legislation. Again, Professor Laveleye
insists on a more concrete treatment of economic subjects than was common with Ricardo and his followers. He believes, as the reader will observe from
the chapter in this book on the method of investiga-
tion, that economic laws are to be ascertained by in-
duction,—by observation of the facts presented by
history, physical science, and statistics. Some results
of this belief are to be found in the frequent historical
references in the present volume. Whatever may be
the difference of opinion among economists on the
question of the proper method in their subject, no
one will deny that this greater attention to the actual
facts of the past and of the present is an advantage.

On some questions of detail, and on some of the
unsolved problems of political economy, Professor
Laveleye differs, inevitably, from other writers; and
his opinions on such questions, though of weight, cannot be accepted as authoritative. But in an elementary
work like the present, questions of this kind are but
little touched on. Such a work must necessarily be
occupied chiefly with a presentation of the great

principles of the science. On these, competent thinkers are agreed; and the fundamental principles of the production and consumption of wealth, of its distribution into wages, interest, and rent, of population, of value and price, of money and credit, of international trade, and of taxation, as laid down in these elements, cannot be disputed.

Some doubtful points are necessarily touched on; and it may be well to point out cases in which the propositions advanced in this volume are to be accepted with qualification. The wages question is still one of the disputed fields of political economy. Professor Laveleye's explanation of the causes that govern the rate of wages, which is the one usually given in German treatises of the present time, is doubtless true as far as it goes; but it hardly gives a complete solution of that difficult problem.

Professor Laveleye, it is well known, has been an earnest advocate of international bi-metallism; and in connection with that question he states, probably too strongly, the objections against a single gold standard, and the reasons in favor of a double standard.

It has already been said that the strong humanitarian spirit of our author sometimes carries him too far ; an instance may be found in the somewhat sweeping statement, on page 96, that it is the duty of the public to indemnify workmen who are thrown out of employment by the introduction of machinery. Again, the connection between the abundance or scarcity of money, and the rate of interest, is perhaps too broadly stated on page 197. But these statements, and others in which economic critics may find flaws, turn very largely on questions of degree or of emphasis, on which there is a natural divergence of opinions, and on which, moreover, Professor Laveleye does not stand alone. In the main, the principles laid down are those accepted by all economists of weight. The clearness and attractiveness of the author's style make his presentation of them especially valuable for those who wish to obtain an elementary knowledge of political economy.

In the supplementary chapter some of the questions which are of great practical importance at the present time in the United States are taken up, and a brief statement is made of the economic principles which apply to them. On practical questions, difference of opinion is inevitable ; and there may be those who will object to some of the conclusions reached in this chapter, especially in regard to the subject of money. The writer has endeavoured to state only such conclusions as are warranted by reason and experience.

F. W. Taussig.

TABLE OF CONTENTS.

BOOK I.

PRELIMINARY REMARKS.

CHAPTER I.

CHAPTER II.

CHAPTER III.

CHAPTER IV.

CHAPTER V.

CHAPTER VI.

BOOK II.

THE FACTORS OF PRODUCTION AND PRODUCTIVE LABOUR.

CHAPTER I.

CHAPTER II.

CHAPTER III.

CHAPTER IV.

CHAPTER V.

BOOK III.

DISTRIBUTION AND CIRCULATION.

PART I.—DISTRIBUTION.

PART II.—THE CIRCULATION OF WEALTH.

CHAPTER I.

CHAPTER II.

CHAPTER III.

CHAPTER IV.

Contents.

CHAPTER III.

CHAPTER IV.

SUPPLEMENTARY CHAPTER.

ELEMENTS OF POLITICAL ECONOMY.

BOOK I.

PRELIMINARY REMARKS.

CHAPTER I.

THE MEANING OF ECONOMIC SCIENCE.

§ 1. Definition and Object of Political Economy.

THE term "political economy," first used by Aristotle in the second book of his *Œconomica,* and then by Antoine de Montchrétien, the author of a *Traité de l'Economie Politique,* published at Rouen in 1615, comes from three Greek words : *Oikos,* house ; *nomos,* law ; and *polis,* city or state. It denotes, therefore, the law, or laws, which ought to direct the administration of property in the state, that is, in society. Such is, in fact, the object of economic science.

B

Human beings have wants, and, when united in societies, observe customs or laws. To satisfy these wants, they have their intelligence and their arms, which they employ in the production of useful objects. How should they be organised, or, in other terms, what laws should they adopt, in order to attain by their labour to the fullest and most rational satisfaction of their wants? This is the problem of which political economy seeks the solution.

Political economy has to do with legislation. It seeks an ideal the same as moral science, law, or politics. Almost all the economical questions that come under discussion are questions of legislation— such as the reform of the laws relating to custom duties, of the land laws, of the laws on currency, of credit, of banking, companies, factory labour, railways, taxation, &c. The justice of these questions must be solved by the study of equity, their utility by the study of statistical and historical facts.

The father of political economy, Adam Smith, defined it perfectly when he said that it proposed two distinct objects: first, to put the people in the way of procuring for themselves an ample subsistence; and, secondly, to furnish the state with a revenue sufficient for the public service.

The very name of Adam Smith's book, *The Wealth of Nations*, shows that the object is to determine what is conducive to the production of wealth, and what hinders such production. As has been well said by Droz: "Political economy is a science whose object is to make comfort as general as possible." Bossuet, again, speaking of politics, said that "their true end is to make life easy and nations happy;" and such is also the aim of political economy.

The doctor ought to know the human body, to diagnose its ailments and prescribe remedies for them, as well as the course of life which will preserve health. This is precisely what the economist has to do for society. He must know minutely the mechanism of the social body, must point out those laws and customs which bring misery upon it, and describe the system most favourable to the creation of comfort by means of labour.

Political economy may therefore be defined as "the science which determines what laws men ought to adopt in order that they may, with the least possible exertion, procure the greatest abundance of things useful for the satisfaction of their wants; may distribute them justly, and consume them rationally."

§ 2. What Political Economy is not.

Political economy is commonly defined as "the science which describes the methods of production, distribution, and consumption of wealth." This definition is altogether inaccurate. The modes of producing wealth are described in industrial manuals or treatises on agriculture; the mode of its distribution is the subject of statistics; the account of its consumption the history of the daily life of the various nations.

Political economy is not an exact science, for it is concerned with the wants of man, which constantly vary, and with his actions, which are free. Neither strict definitions nor methods of mathematical deduction are applicable to it.

Political economy is not a physical science, for it does not deal with commodities considered in themselves, *i.e.*, as material objects, but with the laws that assist the production of these commodities; and these laws are relations of the moral order.

Nor yet is political economy a branch of the natural history of man, for it does not inquire how he arrives at producing what he consumes, but what the institutions are which allow of his doing this to the best advantage.

Again, it is not, as is so often asserted, "the science of labour." Descartes' idea of this latter science is this : " There is a practical science, by means of which, understanding the nature of force and the action of fire, water, air, the stars, the heavens, and all the bodies which surround us as clearly as we understand the various crafts of our artisans, we might in the same manner put these agents to all the uses for which they are adapted, and so make ourselves masters and owners of nature."

The science of labour is technology. Political economy has quite another object. It seeks to discover the laws, whether moral, religious, political, civil, or commercial, which are most favourable to the efficiency of labour. It does not teach us how to cultivate the soil, or to work mines, or to make bread. All this is strictly the science of labour.

CHAPTER II.

THE CONNECTION BETWEEN POLITICAL ECONOMY AND OTHER MORAL AND POLITICAL SCIENCES.

POLITICAL economy is one branch of the group of sciences, the object of which is the study of human societies, and which are known in the present day by the name of *Sociology*.

§ 1. Connection between Political Economy and Philosophy or Religion.

Political economy, regarding man as pursuing the useful, is subordinate to the sciences which regard man as pursuing the good and the true, that is to say, to religion or philosophy. These discuss what are the nature and destiny of man, and the use individuals or societies make of their time and of their property depends on the idea which they form of man's destiny. The doctrines which see in man nothing but a body, and in life nothing but an existence of a few moments, stolen from nothingness, will plunge societies into the exclusive pursuit of enjoyment. Asceticism, on the other hand, for which the body is only a source of sin, and life only a probation, will wish to suppress the satisfaction of the most essential wants, and will urge the individual to annihilate himself in the deserts of the Thebaid, on the pillar of the Stylite, or, in India, in the aspiration after the Nirvana.

Avoiding both these excesses, true philosophy teaches us that man ought to seek the full development of all his faculties : those of the mind first, because the intellectual life is the most essential, but those of the body as well, because it is the instrument of the soul. This object is indicated in the well known maxim of antiquity : *Mens sana in corpore sano (Juvenal,* Sat. xv., l. 356). Hence it follows that while seeking the useful, which is its peculiar object, political economy should never forget that material wealth is a means and not an end—the condition of moral and intellectual progress, not the end of life. On the one hand one must not listen to asceticism which sacrifices the body, nor, on the other, to Sybaritism, which sacrifices everything to the body.

The economist should learn from the philosopher what are the motives of human action, so as to regulate the order of society in such manner that men should be constantly induced to employ their time and their strength to the greatest use. The science of the motives which determine the will ought accordingly to serve as basis for the science of the laws which govern the production of wealth.

§ 2. Connection between Political Economy and Ethics.

The connection between ethics and political economy is close.

"Ethics," says an eminent French philosopher, François Huet, "is the science of moral perfection and worth, just as economy is the science of material comfort and value." Ethics, in fact, determines what are our duties in relation to God, to our neighbours, and to ourselves; and these ideas of our duties ought to govern all the actions of economic life.

Ethics enjoins moderation in our needs, energy and conscientiousness in our work, fidelity to our engagements, thrift and prudence in the use of our income, and regard for justice in our relations with one another. There is not one of these laws that is not an essential rule in economy. Energy in labour insures abundant production; respect for justice, a fair distribution; respect for engagements, abundant credit; the spirit of thrift leads to the creation of capital, and the moderation of desires to a good use of time and property.

In the ethical code you find the true root of economic laws. The good, the end of ethics, and the useful, the end of political economy, without being confounded, are inseparable; for the pursuit of the good is always favourable to the production of

the useful.   Hutcheson, the father of Scotch philosophy, inserted in his course of moral philosophy
(1729–1747) some lessons on *Economics.*   Adam
Smith's book, *The Wealth of Nations*, regarded as
the gospel of political economy, was only a fragment
of a larger work treating of the *Moral Sentiments.*
In his treatise on ideology Destutt de Tracy discusses
political economy as an application of the theory
of will.

Political economy, in its turn, is, as Droz has said,
the best aid to ethics, for it shows the advantages
which result from the practice of virtue, and the evils
which are the inevitable consequence of vice.

In fine, ethics is the science of "The Good,"
political economy the science of goods.   The latter
is thus the application of the former—that is to say,
it is morality in action.   Ancient writers, such as
Xenophon and Aristotle, understood by political
economy certain rules which the state or the individual ought to follow in the pursuit of comfort and
the employment of wealth.   The most erudite of
contemporary economists, M. Roscher, has declared
that the rules laid down by the ancients for the
employment of wealth are the essence of the
whole matter.   In these maxims the relation con-
necting political economy and ethics is conclusively
established.

§ 3. Connection between Political Economy and Law.

At any given moment there is some organisation for societies, which, if respected, would be most favourable to the advancement of the human race. This dispensation is the law—civil, constitutional, economic, international; obedience to this is a duty, and at the same time the highest advantage.

Right, or law, is accordingly the direct, or right, road to good, that is, to the perfection of man and society. In Sanskrit *rita*, in German *recht*, in English *right*, in French *droit*, signify alike the straight or direct road, and right, justice, law. To walk in the right road, or in the path of right, is therefore to do everything which is truly advantageous. Justice and utility lay down the same laws. As a French philosopher, Bordas-Demoulin, has said : "The useful is the practical aspect of the just; the just the moral aspect of the useful." These qualities cannot be antagonistic ; and if they appear to be so, to choose that which is just is to ensure doing that which is useful. On the other hand, what is unjust or immoral can never be really useful. *Nihil utile quod non sit honestum*, was an ancient proverb. " The plan of Themistocles," said Aristides, " is much to our advantage, but it is supremely unjust," and so saying he secured its rejection. Seek justice first, and the rest will be added unto you.

Political economy and law underlie one another.

The man who is ignorant of law will be unable
to fathom political economy; and the man who
is ignorant of political economy will be unable
to trace the sources of law. All the acts of
economic life are exercised under the empire of
civil institutions; and all civil institutions have
economic interests for their final cause. If civil
codes have established rights of property, of inheritance, or of testamentary disposition, the equal
right of succession or the right of primogeniture,
mortgage and terms of prescription, it is because
the legislator has believed that these laws were the
most favourable to the preservation and increase of
wealth. For laws ought to be such that it is to a
man's interest to be always upright, industrious, and
thrifty. Lastly, commercial law, governing the legal
relations arising out of trade, is dictated entirely by
economic considerations.

§ 4. Connection between Political Economy and Politics.

Politics seeks to determine the form of government which, at a given time and for a given country,
will secure in the highest degree the liberty and
well-being of individuals. Political economy, in a
more general manner, seeks to determine the laws
which are most conducive to an abundant production of wealth, its fair distribution, and wholesome
consumption.

These two sciences, therefore, as their names

indicate, have the same end. A good political constitution is the first condition of productive labour
and of the saving that creates capital, in a word, of
economic progress. To this despotism and anarchy
are alike an obstacle. Before promulgating a political
law, the lawgiver should always examine what influence it will have on the increase of the national
well-being. The science of administration, which is
only the application of public law, ought to take
the same principles as its guide.

§ 5. Connection between Political Economy and International Law.

Political economy has given a new basis to international law. In all ancient times, and until the
economists of the last century, the interests of
nations were thought to be antagonistic to one
another; and men believed with Montaigne, that
"the profit of the one is the loss of the other."
Economists have proved, on the contrary, that just
as it is to a merchant's interest to have customers
near him rich enough to pay a high price for his
commodities, so it is to the interest of a nation
to be surrounded by other prosperous nations in a
condition to purchase of it, at a good price, all that
it wishes to sell, and to supply it with an abundance of all that it wishes to obtain. For the popular
maxim : " One man's loss is another man's gain," we
ought to substitute, "One man's loss is every man's
loss." By proving that every one is interested in

the well-being of his fellows, our science has given selfishness as a motive to fraternity, and proved the truth of Béranger's fine lines :

> " Aimer, aimer, c'est être utile à soi ;
> Se faire aimer, c'est être utile aux autres."

It the truths established by political economy were generally understood, there would be no longer either war, or preparation for war ; for the most successful war is always a calamity for the victor as much as for the vanquished. As Scialoja, an Italian economist, has justly said : International justice will be the offspring of economic calculation. The prophet Isaiah uttered the admirable expression : " The work of Righteousness shall be Peace."

§ 6. Connection between Political Economy and History.

Political economy can establish nothing without the aid of statistics and history ; for it is only by consulting these two sciences that it can learn what it seeks to determine ; that is to say, what are the laws which are useful or fatal to nations.

Equally in its turn is political economy indispensable to history, for it alone can discover the causes which have led to the greatness or decay of states. The power of states is proportional to their population and their wealth. The development of population and wealth depends on economic causes.

These, therefore, are the ultimate source of the great events of history.

In history this is the question which dominates all the rest—Why did a given state become great? Why did another given state decline? To this question political economy alone can give a sound answer.

Historians speak of the fatal cycle which empires pass through, growing to greatness at first merely to arrive at final decay. These vicissitudes, or *corsi* and *ricorsi*, as Vico calls them, they explain by saying that nations must pass through the four ages of life traversed by individuals—infancy, youth, manhood, and old age, attended by decrepitude. The comparison, however, does not hold good; for, as generation succeeds to generation, a nation is always equally young.

A philosopher-economist, Destutt de Tracy, explains the economic cause of the fact attested by the historian. "Society," he says, "by securing to every one security of person and property, causes the development of our faculties. This development produces the increase of our wealth; the increase of wealth leads sooner or later to its very unequal distribution ; and this, by bringing back the inequality of power, which society at first limited and was intended to abolish, begets weakness and sometimes final dissolution." (*Éléments d'Idéologie,* pt. iv. c. x.)

Since the fall of states has always been brought

about by the imperfection of laws and institutions producing economic disorder, we may suppose that the progress of social science will allow us to escape from the fatal circle, and will secure to mankind a career of unlimited progress. This is the hope of our time, and probably the destiny of our race.

The philosophy of history, which seeks in the course of events a law of Providence, as with Bossuet, or an inevitable physical law, as with Buckle, is at once chimerical and of little use. That philosophy, however, which should make known the causes which have made certain nations free and prosperous, and others servile and miserable, would be of the greatest use ; for it would teach men what they ought to do and what they ought to avoid.

§ 7. Connection between Political Economy, Geography, and Statistics.

Geography is the description of natural facts, statistics the science of social facts expressed by numbers. These two sciences are the indispensable allies of political economy. For it is by the study of the facts attested by them that the economist can learn the effect of laws, and thus decide whether they are favourable or injurious to the production of useful commodities and the increase of comfort.

For instance : Are small estates preferable to large ? It is statistics that must tell us what is the production of food, the quantity of cattle, the length of roads, the number and condition of the inhabitants—in short, what is the wealth of countries where large and small properties prevail, and thus enable us to compare the results of the two systems.

On the other hand, political economy will suggest the questions to which geography and statistics must find the answer, questions which too often they neglect. For instance, what, in any given country, is the system of property, of succession, the distribution of the soil, the modes of exchange, and so forth ?

§ 8. Laws of Nature in Political Economy.

Economic laws are commonly called natural laws. This is a mistake. The laws of nature, that of gravitation or chemical affinities, for example, are imposed on man just as on the rest of the universe. He must set himself to understand them in order to turn them to account, as he already does in the majority of industries, and especially in the use of steam and electricity.

But the laws with which political economy has principally to do are not laws of nature or natural laws ; they are laws laid down by the legislator. He turns the one to account by obeying them, the other by perfecting them. The one defy the will of man; the others emanate from it.

CHAPTER III.

§ 1. The Meaning of Wealth or Riches

POLITICAL economy is the science of the Useful, or of riches or wealth. We must therefore form an exact idea of what riches consists in.

The word "riches" comes from the Gothic *Reiki*, in Old German *Rike*, in Modern German *Reich*. It is connected with the Sanscrit root *râj*, "to be powerful," whence the title of Indian princes, *rajah*, Latin *rex*, and in German *Reich*, "empire." The *ricos hombres* of Spain were the "great" and "powerful."

Riches or wealth is, in fact, power; the power of getting what one wishes done by other men, either by remunerating them directly, as in the case of servants, or by purchasing the products to which their labour must be applied. In the middle ages a rich man kept in his pay a number of retainers ready to obey him. Thus Warwick, "the king-maker," is said to have constantly maintained more than three thousand persons. In the present day the wealthy command the obedience of even more men; but indirectly, by paying for the commodities they consume.

Wealth, then, may be defined as everything which answers to men's rational wants. A useful service, or a useful object, are equally wealth.

But what is a rational want ? The complete and harmonious development of every human faculty being the object in view, all wants, the satisfaction of which tends to this end, may be considered rational. Psychology, or the knowledge of our intellectual being, will teach us the wants of the mind; hygiene will teach us the wants of the body.

It was long thought that the wealth of nations consisted chiefly in the amount of gold and silver which they could draw to themselves. As this quantity is limited, every state endeavoured to obtain from other states as much of it as possible by bounties, by customs dues, and by regulations restricting trade with foreign countries. Hence arose commercial rivalry, political hostility, and finally open war.

A well-known economist, J. B. Say, remarks that in the seventeenth and eighteenth centuries more than fifty years' war was caused solely by this false idea of wealth. In social science errors are fruitful in evils which afflict mankind and ruin nations.

Many economists have regarded as wealth only such things as can be bought and sold. This is an error, in our view. Wealth is what is good and useful—a good climate, well-kept roads, seas teeming with fish, are unquestionably wealth to a country, and yet they cannot be bought.

"Goods" (nearly synonymous with "wealth") is an admirable word. The supreme good is the subject of philosophy and religion, and "goods" the subject of political economy. In "goods" or wealth must be included all that is good for the advancement of the individual and of the human race.

From this idea of wealth it follows, that besides material riches there is also immaterial riches, such as knowledge, manual skill, or the taste for work. The growth of riches is not an unmixed benefit unless it be accompanied by the growth of justice and morality.

It is the abundance of commodities, and not their money value, which constitutes wealth. The greater the abundance of useful objects the less will be their price and money value; but, meanwhile, real wealth is increased.

§ 2. Wants.

A want is the being without something that is necessary, useful, or agreeable. Want begets desire, and desire action. Action, in this view, is the pursuit of objects desired because they answer to wants.

These objects are good, inasmuch as they are the condition of that development of our nature which is the supreme good. The abundance of goods or commodities constitutes wealth. Man attains to it by labour, which is regulated by reason and directed by knowledge, under the sway of law and right.

Political economy tells us what social laws best enable human labour to satisfy human wants. The science of economy is therefore based on the notion of want. In order to satisfy his wants, man labours and saves, and seeks incessantly to improve the instruments and processes of his labour. Wants, labour, the satisfaction of wants—such is therefore the economic circle, in which nations and individuals are moving day by day and year by year.

Food, clothing, lodging, and furniture are the chief wants of the body. The cultivation of the mind and the moral sentiments, of taste, and of family and social relations, is a want of the moral kind.

The number and nature of rational wants varies with the climate and the state of civilisation. It may be good to satisfy more and more wants, in proportion as the means of producing useful commodities are improved. Still it is not true that the progress of civilisation must be measured by the number of wants satisfied ; nor that it is necessary to the solution of economic problems that they should be constantly multiplying. Ancient philosophy, as well as the Christian code, preached the moderation of wants, in accordance with the fine maxim of Seneca : *Si quem volueris esse divitem, non est quod augeas divitias, sed minuas cupiditates.* If you would make a man rich, you need not increase his wealth, but rather diminish his desires. The economist will not gainsay Seneca.

The time devoted to the creation of superfluous commodities, useless alike to the body and the mind, is time wasted ; and time is the material of life. It should be turned to good account, for it cannot be

recovered. Bodily wants, however refined they may
be, only plunge us doubly into materialism, at the
time when we satisfy them, and at the time when we
are procuring what is necessary for their satisfaction.

To encourage the indefinite multiplication of
wants is to drive humanity into sensualism, which
is the death of virtue, and therefore of liberty.
Aristotle spoke very truly when he said: "The
quantity of things which suffice to make life happy
is limited."   The greatest of human benefactors,
Christ, Buddha, Zoroaster, all lived on little, because
they lived the spiritual life, which is the true one:
The spirit of an apostle in a body inured to all
hardship, a combination of which Socrates and St.
Paul are examples—this is the model which the
economist will recommend.

The end of human existence is not eating and
drinking, but happiness, which is made up of health,
leisure, artistic or intellectual enjoyment, and the
pleasures derived from intercourse with our fellows,
There is no need to deprive either ourselves or others
of everything in order to be always accumulating
more wealth.   This is the error stamped by Juvenal
(viii. 84): *Et propter vitam, vivendi perdere caussas*—
for life's sake to forfeit all that makes life worth
living.

§ 3. False Wants and False Wealth.

By *false wants* I mean wants, the satisfaction of
which carries man farther from his aim, which is the

development of his faculties, instead of bringing him nearer to it.

Commodities consumed by these false wants are false wealth. They are rightly called wealth, for they are bought and sold for large sums. But they are false wealth, for they are of no real good or use. Often they are worse than useless—they are injurious; worse than this, they are fatal.

Alcoholic liquors are condemned by hygiene. They are fatal to health, produce drunkenness and all the vices which accompany it, degrade the man who abuses their use, and plunges him in the mire. Yet every year in France their cost amounts to about 16,000,000*l.*; in England to 20,000,000*l.*; in Belgium to 3,200,000*l.*; and in Holland to quite as much. In Russia the tax on such liquors brings the State 200,000,000 roubles, or 32,000,000*l.*—about one-third of the imperial revenue.

According to calculations made in the United States, in ten years alcohol imposed on the country a direct expenditure of about 300,000,000*l.*, and an indirect expenditure of a similar sum. It has sent 100,000 orphans to the asylums, it has brought 138,000 persons to the prison or the workhouse, it has led to 10,000 suicides, and has made 200,000 widows and 1,000,000 orphans. The total expenditure for civilised countries can hardly be less than 250,000,000*l.*

Opium, which brings those who smoke it to idiocy, annually costs China at least 16,000,000*l.*

The inexplicable habit, borrowed from the savages

of burning a leaf of tobacco between the lips, in order to absorb a certain dose of a highly noxious narcotic poison, costs France every year 14,400,000*l.*; Italy, 5,520,000*l.*; Belgium, 1,200,000*l.*; and civilised countries generally more than 120,000,000*l.* — a moderate price for the 600,000 tons of tobacco which, according to the Austrian statistician, von Neumann-Spallart, are annually consumed. The highest part of the human race accordingly spends some 400,000,000*l.* to poison itself in large or small doses.

Women also pay thousands of pounds for precious stones, which have no other effect than to foster two serious vices—vanity in those who wear them, and envy in those foolish enough to wish to have them.

Throw into the sea the alcohol and opium, the tobacco and precious stones, and nothing will be lost. On the contrary, those who were poisoning themselves and corrupting their minds and bodies will gain much in moral and physical well-being. Things whose destruction improves the condition of mankind cannot be true wealth. If all the money and all the hours of labour which this money remunerates, instead of being devoted, as they now are, to producing hurtful commodities, were devoted to manufacuturing useful ones, how the comfort in the world would increase and the destitution diminish !

CHAPTER IV.

§ 1. Value.

THE value of things is in proportion to their utility, for wealth only merits this name in so far as it corresponds to a want, and thus is useful. Real value, then, does not depend on estimation, but on the property possessed by the articles answering to our rational wants. Nevertheless, there will also be a value depending on estimation, *i.e.* on the opinion of those who desire an object ; and this opinion may give a value to things which do not naturally possess any.

Value is a relation between the physical properties of things on the one hand, and men's needs on the other, and this relation is modified by any change in the needs, even when the qualities of commodities remain the same. Thus fur has a value in the north, because it is needed as a defence against the cold. Beneath the equator it is valueless, because this need no longer exists. Medicines, again, have no value for the healthy man, any more than food has for the sick man unable to swallow it.

The value of things is not, as has been maintained, determined by the labour employed in their production, since there are many things of the same value which have nevertheless cost very unequal amounts of labour; a quarter of wheat, for instance, reaped from a fertile soil, and another quarter reaped from a poor one. Again, there are other things which have required similar amounts of labour and yet are of very different values, as the vintages of choice growths and ordinary wines. Lastly, the value of things changes daily, although it is impossible that any change should have taken place in the amount of labour embodied in them; thus a quarter of corn may be worth much more, or much less, this month than it was last.

Value, again, is not determined by exchange. If I am to exchange my horse for an ox, I must first form an idea of the respective values of the two beasts, and then compare them. Thus the idea of value precedes and determines exchange. An exchange, when made, is constantly criticised in the light of ideas of value, as in the remark, A has sold his house, field, horse, &c., for much above, or below, its value.

The real basis of a thing's value is its utility, *i.e.* the uses to which it can be put, or the wants which it supplies; it is because bread satisfies my hunger that it has a value in my eyes. The greater this power of satisfying a rational want, the greater an object's value. An ox is thus worth ten times as much as a sheep, as giving ten times as much nourishment.

It must, however, be added that the value of a commodity increases in proportion to its scarceness,

and decreases with its abundance, and this for obvious
reasons. The scarcer the commodity, the more
difficult will it be to replace, and the more advantageous to possess. On the other hand, the greater
its abundance, the less profit will it bring its
owner. A loaf is thus of greater utility than a hat,
but of less value, because, as a rule, more easily
replaceable. If, however, bread became scarce and
to replace the stock of it a matter of great difficulty,
as in time of siege, no one would give a loaf to
obtain ten hats. Value is thus determined by the
object's utility, combined with the greater or less
difficulty of replacing it.

To prove that it is inaccurate to maintain that
value depends on utility, it has been pointed out
that while water, which is supremely useful, possesses
no value, a diamond is of great value and of almost
no use. This objection is founded on the vicious
method of argument which employs the same word
to express two different ideas. In saying that water
is supremely useful we speak of water as an element,
that is to say, of the whole procurable volume of it,
and in this sense water is truly supremely useful; but
in this sense it is also of supreme value, inasmuch as
any one, if deprived of it, would give all he possessed
to obtain it. On the other hand, in speaking of
water as of small utility, we are speaking of a fixed
quantity of water, such as a gallon or pint, and in
this case water, it is true, has very little value; but
it is also true that such a quantity of water is of very

small utility, since nothing is easier than to replace
it. Again, in saying that a diamond, which is of great
value, is of very little use, we pass a moral judgment,
undoubtedly well-founded, but very ill-understood.
The diamond possesses the utility of satisfying a
want still very keenly felt among men, the cravings,
namely, of vanity. In this case both the want and
the utility are false, but neither will disappear until
reason and justice have made great progress. Thus,
even in the case of water and diamonds, wherever
there is value there is also utility.

§ 2. Value in Use, and Value in Exchange.

"Every commodity," says Aristotle (*Politics*, I. ix.),
"may be used in two ways, first to help to satisfy the
want to answer which it has been created, and,
secondly, to serve for exchange. Boots are of service
in walking, but they may also, by means of exchange,
serve to procure other objects, such as money, food,
or any other product."

According to Adam Smith, the utility of a thing
in so far as it serves the need which gave it birth,
is its value in use; its utility, in so far as it serves
to procure other objects, is its value in exchange.
Value in use will depend on the services which an
object can be made to render, such as, in the case of
boots, the length of time they can be worn.

Value in exchange will depend on the quantity of
the articles which I desire to exchange already on
the market, and also on the quantity on the market

of the articles I desire to receive and which can be offered in exchange. If there is a large supply of boots and but little money, the value of boots will be less than if there were few of these and an abundance of money.

CHAPTER V.

THE METHOD OF INVESTIGATION.

STUART MILL says that political economy is essentially an abstract science, and its method the *à priori* method; and he maintains that it is constructed on hypotheses completely analogous to those which, under the name of definitions, form the basis of the other abstract sciences.

J. B. Say, on the other hand, remarks : " Political economy has only become a science by becoming a science of observation." Say is right; but not in the sense in which the majority quote him. The economist ought to employ the method of observation in quite a different way from the student of nature or physics. The latter observe facts as nature presents them, and do not dream of changing them. When their task is at an end, that of the economist commences.

The economist observes the motives which rouse

men to action. Then he seeks the conditions in which men must be placed in order that, influenced by these motives, they may attain to comfort by their labour.

Like all animate beings, man seeks to support himself and to reproduce his species; so much the naturalist observes. But what are the ideas and the laws which will induce him to increase the stock of food rather than to multiply his species ? This is the inquiry for the economist. To solve the problem he must study the facts presented by history, geography, and statistics. He marks under the empire of what ideas and what laws societies have been prosperous, and why they have been prosperous ; and under the empire of what ideas and what laws they have been wretched, and why they have been wretched. Man being a reasonable creature, a free agent and capable of improvement, the economist advises him to use this reason and freedom so as to adopt the former and reject the latter.

The true method, then, is this : to observe facts not merely with a view to stating them as the naturalist does, but to deduce from them what laws and what ideas must be adopted in order that men may attain to comfort and subsequently to perfection.

CHAPTER VI.

DIVISION OF POLITICAL ECONOMY.

I NEED bread to feed me. I have to produce it as economically as possible—this is the production of wealth.

A companion has helped me to sow the corn, another to grind it, a third to make the flour into bread. Each ought to have his share in the produce, and we make the division as fairly as possible—this is the distribution of wealth.

When every one has his share he ought to use it as rationally as possible—this is the consumption of wealth.

To determine the social laws which enable wealth to be produced most economically, to be distributed most equitably, and to be consumed most rationally, we must study separately each of the three acts which make up the work of economy.

Accordingly, we must divide the matter with which our science has to deal into three parts :—

1. The production of wealth,
2. The distribution and circulation of wealth.
3. The consumption of wealth.

BOOK II.

THE FACTORS OF PRODUCTION AND PRODUCTIVE LABOUR.

CHAPTER I.

THE PRODUCTION OF WEALTH.

§ 1. Definition of Production.

MAN has many and constantly recurring wants. Guided by the impulse of the desires to which these give rise, he takes certain natural objects and either consumes them directly or fashions them in such a manner as to fit them to satisfy his wants. In a word, he produces.

Man cannot create an atom of matter, but he draws minerals and combustibles from the earth, provisions, textiles, and commodities of all kinds from the cultivated soil, and by fashioning and transporting all these things renders them useful. Production, then, is the creation of utilities.

Those who render services to their fellow-men—the magistrate who enforces respect for the law, the policeman who protects us, the doctor who cures, and the teacher who instructs, are all doing useful work, and thus contribute to production, although their labour is not incorporated into material objects. To render service is, indeed, often more useful to man than to fashion objects, for we do not live by bread alone.

§ 2. The Three Factors of Production.

Production requires the aid of three factors, nature, labour, and capital. A market-gardener produces vegetables ; the field he cultivates is nature, his arms provide the labour, and the implements of husbandry and manure he uses are the capital. Of these factors the first two have preceded and created the third. Quite in the beginning man can be conceived living on the spontaneous products offered by the earth : but soon in order to kill game he would use a stick, or, like Hercules, a club, and, for making dwellings and utensils, chips of flint such as were owned by the prehistoric inhabitants of the lacustrine grottoes and cities. From this time forward capital has assisted labour.

It is principally by the progressive employment of capital and skill that the production of riches has increased. Nature is not more, but less fertile, now than formerly, neither has there been any addition to man's muscular strength : by means, however, of more powerful machines and better processes, man has forced nature to yield him larger products, and so his prosperity continually increases.

CHAPTER II.

NATURE.

In the case of everything adapted to satisfy man's wants nature furnishes the raw material upon which, with the help of capital, labour works, and often also supplies the force which facilitates production. Thus the soil yields us corn, and the waterfall sets in motion the mill which turns the corn into flour. But with every improvement of industrial processes the share of nature in the work of production diminishes, while those of labour and capital increase.

At the outset of civilisation, under such circumstances as still exist in the isles of the Pacific, man was nurtured by nature as a child on its mother's breast; he had but to stretch his hand to take the fruit from the tree, the game in the forest, the fish in the water. To-day, in our great manufacturing towns the aid given by natural agents no longer attracts notice. We only remark the wonders of human labour.

CHAPTER III.

LABOUR.

§ 1. Definition of Labour.

LABOUR is man's action on nature to the end to satisfy his wants.

All living creatures have wants and the means of satisfying them by the use of their faculties; the mollusc absorbs the nutritive elements contained in water; the ruminant browses on grass; carnivorous animals pursue their prey.

In every species there is a proportion between wants and the means of satisfying them; when this relation ceases, the species disappears. Had he been devoid of reason, this must have been the fate of man, since in his primitive condition he appears to have had more wants and fewer means of satisfying them than any other animal. Endowed, however, with an intelligence capable of continuous improvement, man has been able to ceaselessly perfect his means of supplying the wants which have as ceaselessly grown more varied and numerous. A hammer strikes harder than his fist, a knife cuts better than his teeth, a hatchet, even of flint, is far more powerful than his nails. As the methods of his labour improve, it becomes more productive,

D

that is to say, produces more useful articles with less exertion.

Labour, as La Fontaine has told us, is a treasure. It is, in fact, the source of all our wealth. We cannot appropriate to our needs the smallest particle of matter without, at least, seizing it, and in most cases, fashioning it to our use.

Labour is thus a natural law for man, and, as a consequence, a duty. Man has not only a stomach demanding nourishment, he has also arms intended to procure its food. When St. Paul said, "Whoso will not work, neither shall he eat," he only formulated a universal law, the breaker of which wrongs all his fellow-men.

Complete idleness is a fraudulent bankruptcy.

"Idlers," says the old Greek poet, Hesiod, are as the drones which eat up the fruit of the bees labour. Labour will make you dearer both to gods and men, for they hold the idle man in horror." In the book of Job one reads, "Man is made to labour as the bird to fly;" and the Wisdom of the nations also has said that "Idleness is the mother of all the vices." We should not, however, forget that the labour of the hand is not the only, or the most productive, form of toil. The brain produces more than do the muscles.

Man is made for action. As a rule it brings him happiness, and, even in times of affliction, a consolation. Action is indispensable to the health alike of his body and his soul. Inaction, on the other hand, engenders misery in the poor, and in the rich, melancholy. It often happens that a man who leads an active life longs for repose, and when he obtains it finds in it a burden that brings him to the grave. It has been well said by Vauvenargues that " Man only aims at rest as a release from the bondage of labour; but he can have no enjoyment save by action, and this is his only love." In the fine words of a French poet :

> " Nous ne recevons l'existence
> Qu'afin de travailler pour nous **ou pour autrui.**
> De ce devoir sacré quiconque se dispense
> Est puni de la Providence
> Par le besoin ou par l'ennui."

Montesquieu relates a saying of an Emperor of China, "If one of my subjects does not labour, there is some one in my country who suffers from hunger and cold." Since labour is action towards an end, it is always composed of an effort of the muscles guided by an effort of the mind; thus in nailing planks together to make a door, my intelligence directs my arms towards the goal of making a useful object.

The farther industry advances the greater will be the share of intelligence in labour. Compare the carrier employed by explorers in Africa with the engineer who guides a locomotive. The first sweats and toils under a load of half a hundredweight; the second by merely opening a valve sets in motion hundreds of tons.

All labour is a form of motion; man can do nothing save alter the positions of objects. By placing them in what observation has revealed as the more useful positions, he enables the forces of nature to act for him and accomplish the transformations his needs require. I open a furrow with the iron of my plough, and throw into it grains of wheat; moisture and heat set the vegetative properties of the seeds in action: all I have done is to alter positions and I obtain a harvest of wheat. Again, I cast into a blast furnace a mixture of ore, coal, and flux, or calcareous stones. I strike a match and set light to the fuel. Once more there is only a change of positions, but chemical forces are set at work and I obtain iron foundings. In all labour, then, objects must be disposed in such manner as to make the forces of nature lend the greatest possible help to the work of production.

Labour, which is always a duty, can never be a right. The prosperity of human societies depends above all things on the wise direction of labour. Let us examine what is favourable to this.

§ 2. Productiveness ot Labour.

Since labour is always a pain we must endeavour to obtain the maximum of utilities with the minimum of efforts and pains. As a consequence the question how to attain the knowledge of what may lead to this result, in other words of what will increase the productiveness of labour, is the most important

of any in economy. If considered under all its
aspects, it may even be said to include every other.

The causes which increase or diminish the productiveness of labour are very numerous : facts of
nature, human ideas, knowledge, sentiments, institutions and laws. Here, in truth, lies the true field
for the studies of the economist ; it is in this domain
of human liberty that he can point out the reforms
which should be effected, the ideal which should be
pursued. History and statistics supply the facts
from which he draws his conclusions. The subject
is a vast one. Not to diverge too widely from customary methods, I can only touch on it in pointing
out the most important causes which render labour
productive.

§ 3. Responsibility.

Responsibility is the motive power of the economic
world.

Just as the mainspring turns the wheels of a
watch, so the instinctive desire for self-preservation,
for development, and for perpetuation, impels all
animate creatures to economic action, from the
monad, or simple living cellule absorbing in itself
the substances on which it lives, to man in the most
wondrous creations of his industry. The stronger
this spring the greater will be industrial activity ;
and the greater and better directed industrial
activity, the more utilities will then be created, the
greater will be the growth of prosperity.

The problem, then, to be solved, is the means of giving to this mainspring a maximum of force. Its solution is simple : we must assure to every act a treatment proportioned to its deserts ; reward for the good, punishment for the bad, gratification and comfort to the laborious and thrifty, privation and destitution to the idle and prodigal. In this way we apply to economic relations the great principle of distributive justice. The allotments of rewards in schools are an example of the application of the principle. The thing, then, which we have to do, is to organise responsibility. In the case of animals responsibility is brought home in natural ways under the rule of natural laws. The ox which should sleep throughout the day, or the lion which should neglect the chase, would soon die of hunger. Among men, however, where freedom of will is paramount instead of necessary laws, responsibility has to be organised by social laws. The more completely these social laws assure to the labourer the fruit of his labour, the greater will be the incentive towards working long and hard, and the more active will be the mainspring of the economic world.

In his article on political economy in the *Encyclopedia* Rousseau lays down that " The laws should be so framed that labour should be always necessary, and never useless."

§ 4. The Influence of Nature on the Productiveness of Labour.

Some philosophers, such as Montesquieu, Cuvier, and Buckle, have believed that the degree of prosperity to which nations attain, very greatly depends on the influences of nature. Thus Cuvier writes :— "Of varying height and with many branches, small limestone ranges, the sources of numerous streams, intersect both Greece and Italy. Under the shelter of these, in charming valleys, rich in every product of living nature, philosophy and the arts sprang into being, and here mankind witnessed the birth of its most honoured geniuses, while the vast sandy plains of Barbary and Africa have always retained their inhabitants in the condition of roving and savage shepherds." The great naturalist even goes so far as to say, " Granite districts produce on all the customs of human life quite different effects from those of limestone. Board, lodging, and habits of thought will never be the same in Limousin or Basse-Bretagne, as in Champagne or Normandy."

Undoubtedly the constitution of the soil, the conformation of the country, and, above all, the climate, must exercise a great influence on the labours of man, on the produce which he gathers in, and, consequently, on economic progress. A country without mines will produce no metals, and a people living far inland will not be able to devote itself to navigation. Climates, like those of the polar regions, of

excessive cold, or as in the equatorial, of excessive
heat, are not favourable to the productiveness of
labour.   Excess of cold diminishes the activity of
nature ; excess of heat, the activity of man.   It is a
temperate climate that most favours industrial progress.   As has been well said, " Man is here perpetually invited to labour," for here, if nature is generous,
she is so within limits, and only for those who study
and understand her.

The variation of the seasons develops a spirit of
reflection, habits of foresight, and consequently that
creation of capital which is a condition of all
economic progress.   In proportion, however, as man's
empire over nature increases, her influence on his
condition diminishes.   Under the guidance of science
the power of industry in every country turns local
resources to advantage, and, thanks to commerce,
any people can enjoy the products of every kind of
climate.

In the ages of barbarism nature makes man ; in
the ages of civilisation man makes nature.   In the
course of a generation we have seen the same
country, with the same climate, successively occupied
by men plunged in the most abject destitution, and
then by other men enjoying the highest degree of
prosperity.   In Australia, where but lately the aborigines were feeding on carrion and often died of
hunger, magnificent towns, like Sydney and Mel-
bourne, are now rising, ornamented with all the
splendours of civilisation.   In America, on the vast

plains where the Indian would have for ever continued to live in misery on the uncertain products of
the chase, the Anglo-Saxons are every day founding
societies of astonishing prosperity.

Traverse the world, and it will not be in the
countries most favoured by nature that the richest
peoples will be found. It is the right direction of
labour, rather than the fertility of the soil, that contributes to wealth. The value of the land varies
with that of the men who work it; it is the intelligence and energy of the cultivators which make it
precious.

The powers of civilised man are becoming more
and more competent to annul the effects of natural
differences. The conquests of science in their universal diffusion will produce a very similar condition
of civilisation in every country. Montesquieu was
right in his assertion: " Bad legislators are those who
enhance the defects of climate, good legislators are
those who oppose them."

§ 5. Influence of Race on the Productiveness of Labour.

It is impossible to deny that aptitudes and inclinations are different in different races, and that these
are not all equally ready to devote themselves to
labour and the perfecting of its processes. Contrast
the Australian, who will submit to starvation and
misery rather than cultivate the earth, and the
Chinese, who seems to find his happiness in relentless

and unceasing toil. Even among Europeans all
nations do not bring the same aptitudes to their
work. Where energy and perseverance are demanded the English are without rivals. The French
have more taste and dexterity. Americans are the
greatest adepts in the division of labour and the
invention of machinery. If regard be had to the
work done, the Belgian labourer is the least costly of
any. Further, every country has its specialties: in
marble, Italians are the best workers; in zinc,
the Belgians; in iron, the English, and in silk, the
French. Extreme cases excepted, education, habits,
beliefs, institutions and laws—in a word, the causes
susceptible of modification, exercise on the productiveness of labour a much greater influence than do
flesh and blood, *i.e.* than the causes which are
hereditary and unalterable.

Man is never sparing of his pains when these are
properly rewarded. Thus Italians, though they are
accused of idleness, brave the risk of fever in the
Roman Campagna, and reap the corn under the
terrible heat of June. Thus, too, the negro in the
United States, since he has obtained his liberty and
the right to hold property, takes care of his hut and
his crop of cotton; and even in the middle of Africa
the blacks cultivate their fields well whenever they
are in a state of security. In former times, so-
called inferior races, as the Indians of Peru, and the
Aztecs of Mexico, have constructed cities, palaces, and
irrigatory canals, the ruins of which excite astonish-

ment, while they maintained the highest system of cultivation in countries which under Europeans have become impoverished and depopulated. This affords the most convincing proof that in favouring production, institutions and laws are more effective than blood and race.

Since man is capable of perfection, to whatever race he may belong, he can acquire by means of education the greater part of the aptitudes in which he may be deficient.

§ 6. Influence of Philosophic and Religious Doctrines on the Productiveness of Labour.

In proportion as a philosophic or religious doctrine is founded on a just conception of man, his destiny and duties, it is favourable to abundant production of wealth, to its fair distribution and rational consumption. Exactly so far as a philosophy or creed is contrary to reason, it helps to perpetuate misery and injustice. If the economic condition of Christians be compared with that of peoples of other creeds, the difference is at once apparent. Nor can this difference be attributed to the influence of race, since many Mussulmans and Hindoos are whites, while the barbarous and Mohammedan Circassians of the Caucasus are among the noblest branches of our race, which certain writers have even called "Caucasian."

Christianity has been favourable to national prosperity, because by it labour, simplicity of life, and justice in social relations, have been brought into honour. Again, it has put an end to slavery, not by commanding its abolition, but by proclaiming to men that they are brethren and equals. Even while preaching indifference to riches it has opened the sources from which wealth flows. The Christian communities which have followed most strictly the spirit of the Gospel have enjoyed the most widely spread prosperity, and among the Quakers in England, as Voltaire has remarked, and among the Mennonites in Holland, no poor can be found.

Notwithstanding the spiritual elevation of his monotheism the religion of Mohammed, except among the Moors of Spain, has everywhere been opposed to economic progress. Its fanaticism has produced indolence ; its polygamy, the degradation of women ; and the constant theocratic nature of its government a diminution of individual energy.

The religion of China, in which the moral element has longed gained the ascendant over the childish theogony which it contains, has been most favourable to labour by making it a duty, it might even be said an act of devotion. Thus on certain festivals the Emperor himself guides the plough. In Japan, again, agriculture and industry had reached the highest pitch of perfection, unaffected by any European influences. The fields were admirably cultivated, and comfort widely diffused. Shinto, the ancient religion of the Japanese, was a worship of nature of the simplest character, encumbered with few rites and superstitions, and enjoining simplicity and economy not only on the great, but on the Emperor himself, and on all men the duty of work.

The aptitude of the Israelites for self-enrichment is one of the most curious facts in economic history. In former times they converted the barren hills of Palestine into a land "flowing with milk and honey," the comfortable home of a dense population. Since their dispersion, by their accumulation of capital, they have been advancing to the conquest of the world throughout which they are scattered. With their superiority in this respect race can have nothing to do, since their fellow Semites, the Arabs, have offered obstinate resistance to all economic progress. Their success is the consequence of their moral and religious ideas, which have created in them a second nature wholly devoted to the production and capitalisation of wealth. In other ancient countries labour was despised as the lot of a slave; in Israel, on the contrary, the prophets glorified it as the source of all prosperity, while they blamed idleness as the mother of vice and suffering. Manual labour was considered as a means of improvement, and even the learned were obliged to practise it. Sages and their disciples alike guided the plough, and took as their maxim "labour and learn." Here are some extracts from the Proverbs of Solomon :

"He becometh poor that dealeth with a slack

hand, but the hand of the diligent maketh rich"
(x. 4).

"Go to the ant, thou sluggard, consider her ways and
be wise; which provideth her meat in the summer,
and gathereth her food in the harvest" (vi. 6—8).

"Yet a little sleep, a little slumber, a little folding
of the hands to sleep: so shall thy poverty come
as one that travelleth, and thy want as an armed
man" (vi. 10, 11).

The Talmud, on the authority of Psalm cxxviii.,
places the man who works above the merely
pious, and upholds the labour of the hands as
equally honourable with that of the intellect
(Berachot, 17). On this subject some sentences in
the Talmud are truly admirable:

"Great is labour: whoso gives himself to it is
nourished, exalted and ennobled."

"Only he who serves the earth receives its full
bounty."

"Rather gnaw carrion in the streets than have
recourse to charity."

"Whoso teaches not his son a trade brings him
up to be a thief."

Here again is a story from the Talmud: A rabbi,
carrying a plank from his field, was asked if there
were no workmen to save him the trouble. He
replied, "This I do to show the people that labour
is no disgrace. It is only he who shuns it who is
dishonoured." Hence the maxim, "Love labour,
and hate excessive wealth."

The regions of the Tigris and Euphrates, now so desolate, once formed the Persian Empire, renowned in all antiquity for the fertility of its fields and the wealth of its towns. This prosperity was due to the blessing which Zoroastrism, a religion of great purity and elevation, pronounced upon labour. Here are some extracts from the Zendavesta in praise of toil:

"Creator of the corporeal world, Pure One! What is the increase of the Mazdayaçnian law?

"Then answered Ahura Mazda (Ormuzd, God): When one diligently cultivates corn, O holy Zarathustra. He who cultivates the fruits of the field cultivates purity" (Vendidad, iii. § 97—99. Bleek's translation).

"Creator of the corporeal world, Pure One! What is in the third place most acceptable to the earth?

"Then answered Ahura Mazda: Where by cultivation there is produced most corn, provender and fruit-bearing trees; where dry land is watered, or the water drained from too moist land."

"Creator of the corporeal world, Pure One! What is in the fourth place most acceptable to the earth?

"Then answered Ahura Mazda: Where most cattle and beasts of burden are born" (iii. § 11—17).

"He who cultivates this earth with the left arm and the right, with the right arm and the left, O holy Zarathustra! to him it brings wealth.

Like as a friend to his beloved, she brings to him issue or riches " (iii. § 84—86).

" He who does not cultivate this earth, O holy Zarathustra, then this earth speaks to him : Man, thou who dost not cultivate me. Always thou standest there, going to the doors of others to beg for food. Always they bring food to thee, thou who beggest lazily out of doors " (iii. § 91—94).

If some religious doctrines have been singularly favourable to economic progress, certain errors have been productive of great evils. Such is the case with intolerance, that aberration of religious sentiment of which it may be said that it is not only a crime but a mistake—a crime against the majesty of man, and a great mistake in economy. Thus it was intolerance which robbed Spain of the Moors with their perfect system of cultivation, and of the Jews who created its commerce and procured its financial credit. It was intolerance, too, that ruined the Belgian provinces in the sixteenth century, and, after the revocation of the Edict of Nantes, chased from France its most industrious inhabitants. Religious liberty, on the other hand, attracted to Holland refugees and proscribed persons from every country, victims of every kind of intolerance ; it thus contributed greatly to the prosperity of the united provinces.

§ 7. The Influence of the Moral Sentiments on the Productiveness of Labour.

There is not a virtue which does not lead to true wealth, nor a vice which is not an obstacle to well-being. As has been well said, "Moral progress always brings with it an increase of prosperity. But material progress, unless accompanied by an equivalent progress in morality, is always the fore-runner of decline." The circumstances of the downfall of every great empire of antiquity may be cited in support of this truth.

A good conscience in a workman means a good piece of work. When the conscience is bad, the work will be little and ill done. Prudence leads to thrift, thrift gives birth to capital, capital makes labour productive.

Prudence is a mental gift; it is the seeing future events as if they were actually present. "Dig your well before you are thirsty," says the Japanese proverb. Because they foresee needs yet to come, men save a portion of what they produce, and thus collect the means of living in greater comfort and producing more. The spirit of economy enriches, not only families, but states. Prussia, which, in the phrase of Voltaire, was only "the desert of the Marquis of Brandenburg," has become a powerful state, thanks to the spirit of order, economy, and intelligent administration, which imbued its kings, especially Frederick II., while during the same

E

period France was being ruined by the extravagance of the time of Louis XIV., the immorality of the Regency, and all the disorders of Louis XV.

According to Montesquieu, the Caribbees break down a tree in order to gather its fruit. Here we have improvidence personified. From improvidence spring drunkenness and intemperance; these destroy at once the fruits of labour and the aptitude for work, and in this way misery is perpetuated.

Credit is only another word for confidence, and confidence depends on the certainty that engagements will be faithfully observed. Thus this powerful lever of commerce rests on a virtue as its support; where, as in the East, this virtue is not present, credit also is not to be found.

Perseverance, another virtue, is also a great economic force. It is by perseverance that the men of Zealand have justified their assumption of the proud motto *Luctor et emergo* ("I struggle and survive") by twice conquering their territory, the first time from the sea, the second, from the tyranny of Spain. It was perseverance, again, that presided at the birth of the United States, when the first emigrants had to contend against the climate, disease, and the savage tribes.

Administrative venality and partiality in dispensing justice are great obstacles to progress in Russia. Of this the Emperor is not ignorant, but he knows no means of remedying the ill.

As M. Le Play remarks in his *Études sur les*

Ouvriers Européens (p. 4), "The social rank of the different classes of workmen is determined by the degree of development in them of the feeling of prudence." If the Flemish communes were so rich and powerful in the Middle Ages, it was because all the manly virtues of the labourer prevailed among them, assiduity, conscientious workmanship, the spirit of economy, intelligence, carefulness, a feeling of brotherhood among the members of the corporation, and, finally, courage to defend their liberties and privileges.

In his *Survey of Political Economy* Mr. Macdonell makes the following very just remarks: "Wherever there is a great store of wealth there must be a people living under moral restraint and possessed of a code of duty, and a land dotted with bursting stackyards, mapped out into well-tilled fields, and noisy with the hum of looms and clang of hammers, is evidence that there is at hand no small portion of the stuff out of which martyrs and heroes are formed. Though fine names may not be given to the qualifications of a busy people, skilled in many crafts and trades, producing articles cheaply and well, it is patience and sobriety, and faithfulness and honesty, that have gained for them eminence" (ch. **v.** p. 57).

§ 8. The Influence of Justice on the Productiveness of Labour.

" Seek first justice, and all things else shall be added to you." The truth of this quotation from the Gospel can be clearly demonstrated.

Distributive justice consists in treating every man according to his deserts, rewarding the well-doer, punishing the ill. This principle, in the economical order, leads to the maxim, " To every man according to his work." For this maxim to be applied the law must assure to every one the full enjoyment of the fruits of his labour. Let him who sows, reap, and let him who plants the tree, eat of its fruit. You have performed your task with intelligence, zeal and care ; you are entitled to good lodgment, good food, and a provision for your old age. You have been idle and careless; want and famine shall be your punishment. Such is the will of justice. It is the fable of the grasshopper and the ant.

Men have not been wrong when, in confidence in the power of right, they have pronounced the celebrated phrase, *Fiat justitia, pereat mundus* (" Let justice be done, though the world perish "), or when at the time of the French Revolution, in reference to the abolition of slavery, they exclaimed, " Rather perish our colonies than our principle."

What is absolutely opposed to justice can never be favourable to the well-being even of those who seem to profit by the wrong. Thus it was slavery which was the main cause of the decline of the Roman power. In the early days of the Republic the earth was tilled by freemen, and everywhere there reigned a prosperity which, if simple, was real and sound. By dint of constant war this race of well-to-do, brave, and vigorous peasants, gradually disappeared. The aristocracy invaded their little homesteads, as well as the *Ager publicus*, or public land, and formed vast estates, which they cultivated by means of slaves. Livy records this depopulation in an expressive sentence : *Innumerabilem multitudinem liberorum capitum in eis fuisse locis, quæ nunc, vix seminario exiguo militum relicto, servitia Romana ab solitudine vindicant.* . . . ("Vast numbers of freemen used to live in these regions, which now remain a nursery for scarce a handful of soldiers, and are only saved from absolute solitude by the Roman slave gangs.")

Tiberius Gracchus, when on his way to Spain, saw with grief the deserted condition of the fields, and afterwards, in his harangues to the people, painted it in flaming colours: "The wild beasts of Italy have their lairs to which they can retreat, the brave men who shed their blood in her cause have nothing left but light and the air they breathe ; without houses, without any fixed abode, they wander from place to place with their wives and children. They fight and die to advance the wealth and luxury of the great. They are called masters of the world, and have not a foot of ground in their possession."

In spite of the laws of Licinius and the Gracchi, and of all the attempts made to re-establish the class of small proprietors, the process of depopulation did not stop. Rome was supported by the plunder and ruin of the provinces by its proconsuls, and the trial of Verres shows us the hateful brigandage with which these were effected. It was under the weight of the iniquities by which she lived that Rome fell. In the words of Juvenal: *Sævior armis luxuria incubuit, victumque ulciscitur orbem* (Sat. vi. 292). ("A luxury more ruthless than the sword settled upon Rome and avenged the world she had enslaved.") When the barbarians arrived they found the empire almost depopulated.

In the United States the curse of slavery was only extirpated at the price of the most frightful civil war known to history, the death of half a million of men, and the loss of five hundred millions (sterling) of money.

When the injustice of laws reaches such a point, that the hopes of most people are set on robbery, and the most utterly wretched are resorting to crime, the society is advancing towards its ruin. The greater the exactness with which the economic organisation insures the application of justice, the more eagerly will men, who naturally make well-being their aim, betake themselves to labour. To cite a single example : it is to insure this result that patents are granted to inventors, and authors allowed the copyright of their books.

Besides just laws, there must be just judges to apply them. This point is of the first importance. How often do we read in works of history that "justice caused the kingdom to flourish." "*Le royaume multiplie tellement par la bonne droiture,*" writes the chronicler Joinville, "*que le domaine, censive, rentes et revenus du Roy croissent tous les ans de moitié.*" I borrow from Destutt de **Tracy** this wise remark : "Among sensitive beings, whose interests often clash, justice is the greatest of blessings; it alone can pacify them without leaving to any a cause of complaint."

§ 9. Civil Laws, especially those as to Property, in their Relation to the Productiveness of Labour.

Civil laws should be applications of the principles of justice. They must, therefore, assure to every one the enjoyment of that which lawfully belongs to him : *cuique suum*—"to each man his own." Such is, in reality, the formula of justice. From this principle by a direct deduction we reach the most important of all civil institutions, that of property, which we define as the exclusive right to use an article within the limits of reason and law, or, in the admirable phrase of the Roman code, *usque patitur ratio juris.*

Aristotle (*Politics,* i. 3) well characterised property as "an external instrument necessary to man's existence." Property is necessary to man's accomplishment of his destiny, because it is the indispensable complement of his individuality. Property in all the fruits of his work must be guaranteed to the worker. This is the decree of equity, and it is also the decree of the interests of society. It is only the certainty that he will enjoy this legitimate reward of his toil that will impel man to work his best and his hardest. "Make proprietors and you make good citizens," says P. L. Courier. "Nothing can be more beneficial than to give the land to the men who work it: the more an estate is divided, the more it will prosper and improve."

§ 10. Influence of Systems of Inheritance on the Productiveness of Labour.

Differences in the system of inheritance have a considerable influence on men's activity, and on the constitution and progress of societies. Tocqueville (*Democratie en Amérique*, iii. 3) even asserts that "whenever human societies undergo any great change, hidden among its causes is invariably found the law of inheritance."

An analysis of the motives which impel men to production establishes the fact that his daily needs are sufficient to keep the workman to his labour, and in the case of an exceptionally prudent man, to induce him to save a little as a provision for his old age: on the other hand, to bring about great improvements of which the fruits will only be reaped after the lapse of years, the interests of children must be introduced as an incentive. No one will plant trees for a stranger to gather their produce. As La Fontaine puts it, "It is still worth while to build, but to begin planting at my age!" Thus for the creation and preservation of capital the institution of inheritance is an essential.

To maintain and increase the productiveness of labour, is it better that all the real property should pass to one only of the children, as the English law desires, or that it should be shared among them all, as under the French code? The division of an estate may sometimes involve inconveniences, but these are as nothing compared to the immense advantage of making as many families as possible into proprietors.

Property is the condition and complement of liberty. Ideally, every family should have its house, its field, and its instruments of labour, or a title representing a share in a common capital—a factory, for example, or some other enterprise. By the regulation of inheritances this ideal is attainable.

§ 11. Influence of Systems of Tenure on the Productiveness of Labour.

Lands are cultivated sometimes directly by their owner, sometimes by other persons to whom he grants the occupation of them under such different conditions as métayage, leasage, emphyteusis, &c. Modes of tenure are favourable to production

in proportion to the completeness with which they
assure to the cultivator both the fruits of his labour
and the benefit of his improvements. Thus tested,
no system is equal to that of absolute proprietorship.
Arthur Young, an economist of the eighteenth century well versed in agriculture, says, "Give a small
proprietor a strip of rock, and he will make it into a
garden. The magic of property turns sand into
gold." In the Pyrenees, in Tuscany, on the slopes
of the Apennines, or at Capri, that shelf of calcareous rocks at the entrance of the Gulf of Naples,
famous as the retreat of Tiberius—in all these places
the traveller will see the soil actually created by
man's labour. Terraces of unmortared stones are
constructed on the hill-sides : to these earth is
carried in baskets, and often is carried afresh after
each violent storm. Vines and olives are then
planted, and at the foot of these grow corn and
lupine. The proprietor has created his property
by the sweat of his brow, and affords us an example
of what men will do when they are assured of the
exclusive enjoyment of the fruits of their toil.
Again, Arthur Young tells us that, "with a yearly
tenancy a farmer will ruin the finest soil," and the
misery of the Irish and their wretched system of
cultivation are his proofs. The cultivator cannot
be expected to improve the soil if an increase of
rent continually comes to rob him of the results
of his improvements. As means of forwarding
agricultural progress, hereditary tenancy, emphy-

teusis, and long leaseholds compete the more closely
with actual proprietorship in exact proportion to the
greater security and permanence of the tenure. A
scale of the different systems of land tenure may
thus be formed, arranged according to the encouragement which they give to labour. The order will
be, in descending scale :—

(1) Proprietorship vested in the cultivator.
(2) Hereditary tenancy or emphyteusis.
(3) Long Leaseholds.
(4) Métayage.
(5) Short leaseholds.
(6) Tenure at will.

§ 12. Influence of Systems of Rewarding Labour on its Productiveness.

Man will work with so much the more care
and zeal the more exactly his reward is in proportion to the quantity and quality of his labour.
Pay the industrious and the idle workman the
same wages and it will be to the interest of
both to do as little as possible. Since activity in
labour is thus in proportion to the strength of the
motives which result in it, labourers, compared in
this respect, can be arranged in the following
descending scale :—

(1) Those who keep for themselves all they produce.
(2) Those who have a share in the profits.

(3) Those paid according to the work done.

(4) Those paid according to the time they are supposed to be working.

(5) Slaves, the produce of whose labours belongs to their masters.

The small proprietor is already in his fields before the dawn, and at sunset he is still toiling; the harvest, that is to say his welfare, depends on his industry. On the other hand, the idleness of government officials is proverbial, and it is so, because they are treated the same whatever quantity of work they do. Lastly, slavery, by taking from man his rights of property as well as of liberty, has blighted his labours with barrenness, and it was slavery which formed the principal obstacle to material progress among the peoples of antiquity.

§ 13. Influence of Systems of Government on the Productiveness of Labour.

"Riches," said J. B. Say, in 1803, "are absolutely independent of political organisation." In this opinion he was profoundly mistaken. Nothing is more favourable to the production of wealth than a good government, nothing more fatal than a bad. To this the history of all countries and of all eras bears witness, and its lessons are better understood by Montesquieu when he tells us "countries are not prosperous by reason of their fertility, but by reason of their liberty;" and by Tocqueville, who writes,

" I do not know that a single example can be cited, from the Syrians to the English, of a manufacturing and commercial people which has not also been a free one. There is thus a close tie and necessary relation between these two things, liberty and industry."

Liberty is the daughter of reason and the mother of wealth.

Despotism finds its ordinary result in decay. Never has this been better exemplified than in the fall of the Roman Empire. "Thanks to the multiplicity of functionaries," says Lactantius, "there were more tax-consumers in the Empire than taxpayers, so that the cultivator was ruined by the exactions to which he was exposed. Fields were deserted, and lands, once tilled, abandoned, till they lapsed again into the forest." "The *Fiscus*," says Salvienus, writing in the sixth century, "was a robbery which completed the ruin of the Roman Empire."

Order, security, liberty, justice, above all, that organisation of responsibility which assures to the industrious the fruits of their labours—these are necessary conditions of the development of wealth ; and a government will advance this development in proportion as it guarantees these conditions. When, as under the old *régime*, taxes fine the workers and savers, without touching those who squander at court the money torn from the cultivators, under such a government prudence is shown in doing nothing and living from hand to mouth. When, as in Turkey, the arbitrary exactions of the treasury increase in proportion to the outward signs of prosperity, to be or to appear poor is the sole guarantee of safety.

To be convinced that a bad government is the worst of scourges it is only necessary to visit the Turkish provinces, formerly the richest in the Roman Empire. "The populations of these provinces," says a traveller, Dr. Lennep, "capable in themselves of great progress, are stifled in a general atmosphere of malversation and decay. Beggars are everywhere; from top to bottom of the social scale there is mendicity, theft and extortion. Little work is done at present, and there will be less in the future. Commerce is degenerating into peddling, banking into mere usury; every undertaking is a fraud; politics are an intrigue, and the system of police sheer brigandage. The fields are deserted, the forests devastated, mineral riches neglected, and the roads, bridges, and all public works falling into ruin." The grass withers in the footprint of the Turk, not because the Turk is worse than his neighbours, but because the Turkish government is detestable.

In the reign of Louis XIV. the same cause produced the same effects. The Maréchal de Vauban, of whom Saint Simon said that he was "the most honest man of his time, with a passion for the public good amounting to madness," wrote, " If any one is well off he must hide what little comfort he

has so carefully that his **neighbours** have no knowledge of it. He must even push precaution so far
as to deprive himself of necessaries lest he should
appear to be in easy circumstances " (*La Dime
royale*).

We pray in the Litany to be delivered from
" plague, pestilence, and famine," and from " battle
and sudden death," but these are only passing evils,
soon repaired by the fruitfulness alike of labour and
marriages. A bad government is a permanent evil,
and, so long as it lasts, the ills it produces go on
increasing. Montesquieu has expressed himself admirably on this point. " There are two kinds of
poor people," he tells us, " the first made so by the
harshness of the government, and thus incapable of
almost any virtue, since their poverty is part of their
slavish lot ; the second only poor because they have
despised or never known the conveniences of life,
and capable of great things since their **poverty** is
a part of their freedom " (*Esprit des Lois*, xx. 3).
Elsewhere, to explain how liberty enriches a people,
the same author writes, " As a general rule a nation
which is in bondage works rather to preserve than
to acquire, a free nation rather to acquire than
preserve."

§ 14. Influence of Democracy on the Produc-tiveness of Labour.

In passages not easily forgotten Tocqueville has
shown the influence which democracy exercises on

the production of wealth.   " Every cause," he writes,
" which gives force in the human heart to the love
of the goods of this world, helps to develop commerce
and industry.   One of these causes is equality; and
this favours commerce, not directly by giving men a
love for business, but indirectly by strengthening and
extending in their minds the love of comfort."

Despite the turmoils inseparable from freedom,
the democratic communities of Greece, of Flanders,
and of Italy, all enjoyed exceptional prosperity and
great renown.   The Florentine historian, Machiavelli,
gives as the reason that "the virtue, morality, and
independence of the citizens were more effective in
strengthening the state than their dissensions in
weakening it.   A little agitation lends energy to
the mind, and the real promoter of human prosperity
is, not so much peace, as freedom."

Slavery brings about decay by diminishing activity.
" When everything rests crushed beneath the yoke,"
says Rousseau, " it is then that everything perishes
and that the chiefs destroy the people."   " *Ubi solitudi-*
nem faciunt, pacem appellant—they make a wilderness
and call it peace " (Tacitus).

§ 15. Influence of the Freedom of Labour upon its Productiveness.

Guided by self-interest, where he has any light,
man will devote himself to the most profitable form
of labour.   It follows that the more labour is free,

the more it will be productive. **Freedom of labour** comprises :—

(1) **Freedom** to choose a trade. **Of** this monopolies and guilds are the negation.

(2) Freedom to labour wherever one pleases : no privileges for certain districts; freedom in the choice of a dwelling.

(3) Freedom of partnership.

(4) Freedom to buy and sell to the best advantage : freedom of trade.

(5) **Freedom** to lend money : abolition of the laws against **usury**.

All these liberties, proclaimed by the French Revolution and adopted in England, have since the end of the last century successively gained a footing in the different civilised countries. Hence has resulted an extraordinary increase in the activity and productiveness of labour.

Nothing contributes so much to render labour productive as the free competition of the labourers. It is a pacific contest to see who will sell the most and with the greatest profit. Every one is on the alert, racks his brains, and tries to devise some saving, some improvement, or some new piece of machinery. The punishment of those who fail is embarrassment or misery ; the reward of the successful comfort and wealth.

Among animals the struggle for existence is decided by strength of claws and teeth ; among

F

barbarians by the sharpness of hatchet and javelin; among civilised men by superiority in labour, in invention, and in capital.

§ 16. Influence of Association and Co-operation on the Productiveness of Labour.

To extinguish a fire twenty or thirty men stand in a line, forming a chain from the water to the place of the conflagration; with one hand they quickly pass along full buckets, and with the other return the empty ones. In this way they convey twenty times the amount of water that could be brought by each man running between the fountain and the burning building; and here we have an illustration of the advantages offered by association.

If a boat has to be launched ten men successively pushing will never stir it; if they all push together she is floated at once. Here we have an illustration of the advantages of co-operation.

When arranged in an intelligent and orderly fashion men succeed in doing what a hundred times the number of isolated individuals would never accomplish. This important truth is symbolised by the Roman emblem of a *fascis* or bundle, and by the Austrian device *Viribus unitis*, "By united strength."

The division of labour is based upon spontaneous co-operation. The baker who supplies the teacher with bread, and the teacher who instructs the baker's children, are co-operating in a common work—the furnishing man with the food of the body and the food of the mind. Although they neither know nor intend it, in reality they are partners.

§ 17. Influence of the Division of Labour on its Productiveness.

The division of labour consists in parcelling out a piece of work among those who have to execute it, in such a manner that each workman shall always do the same work, or even only a part of the work. A blacksmith forges nails all the year, and with these nails procures, by means of exchange, everything he needs. This is the first form of the division of labour.

Again, eighteen different operations are needed to make a single pin, and each of these is intrusted to a special workman. This is the second form of the division of labour.

The principle of the specialisation of functions is of spontaneous application. Every one is disposed to do the work for which he has an aptitude, and everybody else profits by his doing it. In the simplest form of life, as seen among savages, the man devotes himself to hunting, the woman prepares the food and clothing.

As human industry progresses, though most of the work continues to be done in the bosom of the family, certain separate occupations make their appearance, such as those of the blacksmith, the worker in copper, and the potter. Still later, speciality of occupation, when combined with hereditary succes sion, as in Egypt, gives rise to caste ; when, as in the Middle Ages, with privileges, to craft guilds.

The division of labour greatly increases its productiveness, and thus proportionately diminishes the price of produce. Pins at from sixpence to ninepence a thousand, playing cards for sixpence a pack, watches for from twelve shillings apiece, are all examples of this cheapness, which will seem wonderful on reflection. These advantages of the division of labour proceed from different causes, of which the following are the chief :—

(1) Increase of skill in the workman from repeating the same process.

(2) Saving of the time lost in getting to work, whenever the occupation and tools have to be changed.

(3) Economy effected in the use of tools, since each workman now only requires one, whereas, when there is no division he needs a different tool for each several operation.

(4) More advantageous employment of the different aptitudes of the workmen, since each is constantly employed on what he does best ; and a notable saving in the cost of labour, inasmuch as where all payments are in proportion to the difficulty of the work, the simpler processes can be intrusted to weaker or less skilful hands, often unhappily to those of women and children, and so are less highly paid.

(5) More frequent employment of machinery to

replace the workmen, wherever any part of the work can be reduced to an identical and regular movement.

(6) The tendency of division of labour to promote equality by a balance of functions. If the strong and the weak are set to the same work the strong will accomplish twice as much as the weak, and, since the fruits of labour are its legitimate reward, will be twice as well off. On the other hand, if they agree to divide their labours between them, the strong man will cultivate the earth for both, the weak will prepare the food and clothing, also for both. In this way, in the first place, both will be better fed and better clothed, and, in the second, since the services each renders to the association balance, they can be equally rewarded. Where advantage is taken of the diversity of men's aptitudes, these can be made to contribute equally to the general production.

The division of labour can be applied with the greater completeness according to the greater extent of the market for the produce, the facility of exchange, and the perfection of the means of communication. In a village where the customers are few the farrier will do all kinds of work in which iron is employed. In a large town, work in iron will be divided among the farrier, the stove-maker, the locksmith, and the makers of tools and safes.

When roads are bad and ill-protected, exchanges are infrequent and difficult, and every group of

men has to produce on the spot everything which
it consumes.   In the villas of Charlemagne the
estate provided food, the women spun and wove
the wool and flax for clothes, and men made their
own tools and agricultural implements.   Nowadays,
thanks to railways, steamers, and the good understanding that prevails among nations, the whole globe
forms a single market, and in the workshop of the
world every nation has to apply itself to furnish the
produce which the soil and climate allow it to obtain
at the smallest cost.

The market for a given class of goods, that is to say
the portion of the world within which they can be
sold, is of less or greater extent according to the
bulk and weight of the goods when compared with
their value.   The market for coal is limited because
the cost of transport is great.   The market for
watches and silks embraces the whole world.

Men have not all the same aptitudes, and, in
harmony with this, different aptitudes are required
by different tasks.   In each kind of labour, then,
a workman should be employed endowed with the
faculties this labour requires.   Iron should be forged
by strong arms; a watch spring be constructed
by a workman with delicate fingers; carving in
wood be done by a man with taste; the direction
of an enterprise be intrusted to the thoughtful
and educated; in this way labour will attain a
maximum of productiveness.   According to our
English maxim we shall have "the right man in

the right place," or, as Cicero long ago perfectly expressed it : *Ad quas res aptissimi erimus, in iis potissimum elaborabimus*—" We shall be choosing for our occupation the employments for which we are best fitted."

In order to attain to division of labour between geographical regions, we must apply free trade between the different countries. From each of these we should demand the products for which nature has given it special advantages : tea from China, coffee from Brazil and Java, iron from England, wine from France, wheat from the black lands of the Danube and of Russia, from the United States cotton, from India rice. In this way mankind in general will obtain the most abundant satisfaction of its needs in exchange for the smallest amount of effort. Division of labour when applied to the whole globe makes all men partners in the universal workshop from which there issues the ever-increasing welfare of mankind.

Alarm has been felt at the consequences of the division of the details of labour. What is to become of the workman who shall devote his whole life to making pins' heads ? This was the indignant question evoked by Adam Smith's now classic illustration. This idea is elaborated by Tocqueville with his usual profundity. " In proportion," he writes, "as the principle of the division of labour receives more complete application, the workman will become more and more feeble, limited, and dependent. If art progress, the artisan will retrograde. The employer will approach ever more nearly to the administrator of a great empire, the workman to the condition of a brute. The difference between them will increase every day" (*La Démocratic en Amérique*, vol. ii. p. 20). Happily the fears Tocqueville expresses have not been realised.

The division of labour cannot be carried very far in agriculture, inasmuch as the tasks to be performed, the sowing and reaping, succeed one another. Yet the agricultural labourer is far from being more intelligent than the manufacturing; and it is in manufactures where the division of details is pushed to an extreme, in the making of watches and fire-arms, for instance, that the most intelligent workmen are to be met. It is very fortunate that this is the case, since the workman must never be sacrificed to the perfecting of the work, inasmuch as the goal to be attained is the improvement and welfare of the human race, and not the mere increase of wealth.

Nowadays, however, specialisation seems carried too far. He who works with his hands should be left some leisure for head-work; and he who works with his head should have some hours for manual labour. Thus Mr. Gladstone cuts down trees, and Lincoln, the President of the United States, used to chop wood. To insure health both of body and mind, both the one and the other must be given proper food and exercise.

The advantages of the division of labour were remarked by the ancients. Plato, Xenophon, and Dionysius of Halicarnassus all speak of them. Plato praises the Egyptians for having always intrusted the same kind of work to the same workman, thereby making him more skilful; and we read in his *Republic* (book ii.): "Would things go better if each man had several crafts, or if each confined himself to his own? Obviously, if each man confined himself to his own."

The following passage from the *Cyropædia* shows that Xenophon perfectly understood the advantages of the division, and even of the sub-division, of labour, as well as the causes which occasion or restrict it. "In small cities the same workman makes beds, doors, ploughs, and furniture; and often even builds the houses. A workman occupied with so many tasks cannot succeed equally well in all. In a large town, on the other hand, where a number of the inhabitants have the same needs, a single craft will suffice for an artisan's support. Sometimes even he will only exercise one part of his craft, as when one shoemaker makes soles for men and another for women; or one gains a livelihood by stitching them, another by cutting them out. According to the nature of things a man whose toil is limited to a single kind of work will excel in this kind."

§ 18. Influence of Science Applied to Manufacture on the Productiveness of Labour.

Virgil sang, *Felix qui potuit rerum cognoscere causas*—"Happy is he who has knowledge of the causes of things," and, in very truth, the better he knows them the better he will be able to profit by them to his own advantage. In the words of Bacon, "Knowledge is power," or as the French philosopher, Victor Cousin, expresses it : "In intelligence we have the primitive capital which contains and produces all others."

Nothing contributes more to increase the productiveness of labour than the application to it of science, that is to say of observation of the facts and laws of nature. Of this the history of economic progress furnishes a proof at every step..

Primitive man observes that in the forest two dry branches when rubbed against each other by the wind, ignite. Imitating the operations of nature, he bores a hole in a piece of light, dry wood, and in this hole turns the point of a piece of very hard wood rapidly round till a flame shoots up. Here we have the discovery of fire, perhaps the greatest which man has ever made, a discovery which at once raised him above the level of the animals. Of the point of wood he has made an emblem to be worshipped, and of the flame a supernatural power—among the Aryans the god Agni. The

Prometheus of the Greeks, who stole fire from heaven, is the *Pramatha* of primitive India, the point of wood, the rotation of which creates the flame (from the Sanskrit root *math*, " to rub "). At Rome the sacred fire was kept up by the vestals, and the same is the case in Peru. It may only be relighted by means of the friction of sticks of wood.

A man picks up a flint and makes it into a hatchet. With this tool in his hand he sallies forth to conquer the world, as do the American squatters to this day. Later on he observes that a bent branch, with its two ends tied with a string, possesses an elastic force which hurls a dart to a long distance. Here we have him armed with a bow, with which he procures much more game than with the boomerang—the sole weapon known to the Australians and to prehistoric men. Again, he sees a tree floating on the water, and concludes that by hollowing it out he can place himself in it and move along the surface of the waves. He does so, and navigation is invented. Once more he perceives that by fashioning the pieces of stone with which he meets into particular shapes, he can use them to hollow wood and to wound and kill animals; he thus makes himself knives, saws, and javelin heads, either in flint or obsidian. After a long interval of time he learns the use of metals, and replaces these tools and weapons of stone, at first by copper and bronze, afterwards by iron. In this way, after an incalculable series of happy chances, observations, deductions, and trials of every kind, man has arrived at the possession of a metal hatchet or arrow-head. It is from this point that the industry of civilised aces, really dates. Starting from this, observations are grouped. together systematically till they become sciences, and chemistry, physics, mineralogy, and mechanics multiply their discoveries, and water, wind, steam, and electricity lend to man's feeble arms the aid of their colossal powers.

Every process of production in agriculture, in manufactures, and in the means of transport is continually being perfected by the application of new scientific discoveries. The progress of the useful arts may be summed up in the single sentence, " every industry becomes a science." A comparison of the widely different degrees of welfare enjoyed by different races confirms the truth of this observation. The savages of Australia live in the most terrible destitution in the same country in which Englishmen are overflowing with wealth. The former know only how to use their hands, the latter, under the guidance of science, oblige the forces of nature and properties of matter to help them in production. The inhabitants of the United States are in every respect better provided than those of Brazil. They make greater use of machinery and scientific processes than do the Brazilians, and this because among Americans knowledge is much more widely diffused.

Progress in the social sciences, philosophy, morals, law, **political** economy, and politics, enables man to gain a better knowledge of himself, to fulfil his duties, to respect justice, and to organise society. It thus helps to favour the production of wealth fully **as** much as do the natural sciences. Hence we **may** conclude **that** a country desirous of increasing **its** prosperity should cultivate **all the** sciences, and **shrink from no sacrifice** necessary **to** forward their advance or **diffuse** the knowledge of their discoveries.

§ 19. Influence of Instruction and Education on the Productiveness of Labour.

This point has been admirably elucidated by an Italian economist, Luigi Cossa. Instruction and education aid in **increasing** the productiveness **of** labour by augmenting, and, **still more,** by giving a better direction to the employment of **man's** powers. To this end there is needed in the first place a general and "humane" education; in the second, one of a more special **and** professional character. In each of these the bodily, mental, and moral faculties must alike be exercised and cultivated.

The bodily faculties are maintained and improved by hygienics and by gymnastics, as the Greeks of old so admirably understood. Thus in the Apologue of Procidus, Virtue says to Hercules, "Do you wish your body to be strong? Remember to accustom it to the governance of the soul, and to exercise it amid fatigue and sweat."

Intellectual culture, in so far as it aims at increasing the productiveness of labour, in the first place, must exercise the attention, the memory, and, above all, the reasoning powers; in the second, must instil a knowledge of the laws both of the physical and moral world, which wield so great an influence over economic activity. Lastly, the cultivation of the moral faculties should stimulate the practical virtues, such as the love of work, forethought, and the spirit of thrift; combat vicious inclinations, such as idleness and prodigality, and aim at strengthening the whole character so as to overcome the obstacles of every kind which impede the path of industrial progress.

To diffuse professional education special institutions must be organised, such as schools of mines, colleges of agriculture, and technical and industrial schools of all descriptions. Every expense incurred with this object will be repaid a hundred fold by the increase of wealth. For the vast majority of men, however, as J. S. Mill remarks, the greater aim of all mental cultivation should be the development of that common sense which will teach a sound appreciation of the circumstances amid which they live, and of the consequences which wait upon their actions.

As an illustration of the manner in which the ancients understood mental and bodily education, we may cite the example of Marcus Aurelius. This emperor went about his palace in the robe of a philosopher, slept on a skin stretched on the earth, studied philosophy, jurisprudence, rhetoric, geometry, and music, and at the same time devoted several hours in every day to such bodily exercise as tennis, running, riding, wrestling, and even boxing.

§ 20. Obstacles Opposed by Ignorance to the Productiveness of Labour.

If it be true that knowledge is the principal source of our welfare, the greater part of our misfortunes must be caused by ignorance. Remembering how earnestly man pursues his good, it is plain that did he know clearly in what it consists, and above all how it is to be reached, he would certainly attain all the happiness of which life on this earth is capable. But amid the intricacies of social life, man fails to discern where his true interest lies, and, too often, when there are no just laws to oppose him, he is ready to sacrifice the good of others to his own selfishness.

Among carnivorous animals the strong devour the weak. Among men, since cannibalism has proved insufficient, the strong have found a more profitable way of using the weak than eating them, this is, to force them to labour, while depriving them, by different methods, of the fruits of their toil. Hence come slavery, war, revolutions and all

the train of miseries which wickedness and violence
have let loose upon mankind.

In ancient times robbery was held the most
honourable way of acquiring wealth. This is plainly
shown by a passage from an heroic song of Tyrtæus,
the patriot poet of Greece. "Everywhere," he sings,
"we reign as masters. Wherever we approach all
things are ours. We reap the vintage with our
lances, our labour is done by our swords." Aristotle
considers war and slave-hunting as legitimate
methods of acquiring wealth. "The art of war,"
he writes, "is a natural method of acquisition.
War is a kind of hunt for such beasts and men as
are born to obey, and yet refuse to be enslaved"
(*Politics*, i. 5). In a phrase, stamped with all the
sharpness of a Roman medal, Tacitus shows us the
same idea prevailing among the Germans : *Nec arare
terram aut exspectare annum tam facile persuaderis,
quam vocare hostem et vulnera mereri. Pigrum quin
immo et iners videtur sudore acquirere quod possis
sanguine parare* (*Germania*, xiv.).—" Nor are they
as easily persuaded to plough the earth and
to wait for the year's produce as to challenge an
enemy and earn the honour of wounds. Nay, they
actually think it tame and stupid to acquire by the
sweat of toil what they might win by their blood."
Despite the high aptitudes of their race and the
excellence of their political and communal institutions, the Germans remained barbarians until the
introduction of Christianity. Robbery maintained

a perpetual state of war both between peoples
and tribes, just as among the Redskins of North
America.

Throughout antiquity, and, despite the teaching
of the Gospel, throughout the Middle Ages, the
sword of the warrior was glorified, and the labourer's
hoe despised. All these fatal errors still linger in
men's minds, and from them proceed national
antagonisms, war, and the spirit of war, and that
curse, perhaps the greatest of all, an armed peace.
This armed peace, it has been calculated, if the loss
of the labour of some three millions of soldiers and
sailors be included, costs the civilised countries some
four hundred millions sterling a year. What a
fruitful source of misery would be dried up if nations
could be led to understand that they have no
interest in ruining and enslaving themselves in
order to filch a province or an estuary! A single
error expelled from the brains of men, and, above
all, of sovereigns, would suffice to transform the lot
of mankind.

The obstacles to international trade, wars of
tariffs, the unproductive and immoral expenditure
of private persons, the abuses of speculation, the
misconception of charity, bad taxes, the vicious
distribution of wealth, the ill uses to which it is
put by states and unions—all these are so many
impediments to welfare which find their causes
in as many economic errors. Peace, justice, and
brotherhood are to the interests of all: as soon as

G

this truth shall be more clearly perceived, the causes of misery will diminish. Whoever is anxious for man's welfare should strive to dispel ignorance and root out error.

CHAPTER IV.

GROSS PRODUCT, NET PRODUCT, AND THE COST OF PRODUCTION.

GROSS product is the total of all the commodities produced by an individual or nation; net product, the amount which remains available, when deduction has been made for the consumption necessary to create fresh gross product. This deduction, these necessary advances, constitute the cost of production.

I harvest a hundred quarters of corn—this is my gross product. But in order to obtain a similar crop the next year, I must keep myself in food, and pay for clothing, hire of tools, manure and other articles I consume. These will cost me the price of fifty quarters—here we have my cost of production. Deducting then from my crop of one hun !red quarters, fifty quarters for expenses, I shall have left fifty quarters, and these constitute my net product.

The productiveness of an industry varies with the amount of its net product; but, as Adam Smith has remarked, it is the gross product which is the more important for the nation, for it is on the mass of

commodities destined for consumption that the
nation is supported. By dividing, in the case of
any country, this total mass by the number of the
population, a figure will be obtained which will give
an idea of the average of individual welfare. The
net, as distinguished from the gross product, is the
support of all persons not directly engaged in any
business, such as stockholders, officers of government, doctors, barristers, &c. It is in England that
this net product is greatest, for it is in this country
that the greatest number of people are found outside
the occupations which have directly to do with
matter. The net produce of a nation is that part
of the total produce which is not necessary for
reproduction. It is this part which economy
can *capitalise, i.e.* turn into capital by using it
to create fresh instruments of labour: it is this
part which is so often frittered away in foolish
extravagance.

CHAPTER V.

CAPITAL.

§ 1. Different Kinds of Capital.

THE third factor in production is capital, which
may be defined as any product of labour saved and
employed for fresh production. Capital is thus, as
has been said, accumulated labour. A spade, a saw,

a plough are all capital : men's hands have made them, and now employ them for the creation of commodities.

All wealth is not capital. Thus the earth, our chief riches, cannot be reckoned as capital, since it is not the work of man. A beautiful hunter is wealth ; it is not capital, since it is not employed in production. It is the character of the employment which determines whether a thing is or is not capital. Thus the same horse, if used for carrying letters, becomes capital, since it contributes to the production of commodities.

Capital is not productive of itself. Labour is the only active force. But labour cannot produce abundantly without the help of capital. If a man scratched the earth with his nails, he would never draw from it a subsistence ; but armed with the spade or plough he need want for nothing. The qualities, aptitudes, and knowledge of the con-tributors to production may be considered as immaterial capital, since they are the results of past labour applied to new. Labour, which is often called "the poor man's capital," is not really capital. Labour is an act, capital the result of an act.

Capital is divided into *fixed* and *circulating*. Fixed or sunken capital is capital not consumed in each operation of production. It subsists, is used for successive operations, only renews itself slowly, and yields a profit without changing owners. This kind of capital comprehends : (i.) buildings destined for manufactures; (ii.) machines and implements; (iii.) improvements absorbed by the soil, such as inclosures, hedges, galleries in mines, &c.

Circulating or floating capital is consumed at each operation and reappears transformed into new products. At each sale of these products the capital is represented in cash, and it is from its transformations that profit is derived. Floating capital includes: (i.) raw materials destined for fabrication, such as wool and flax; (ii.) products in the warehouses of manufacturers or merchants, such as cloth and linen; (iii.) money for wages, and stores.

On a farm the implements of husbandry and beasts of draught that work them are the fixed capital; the cattle for sale, the crops and the money in the cash-box, the circulating. The difference between the two forms of capital depends on the destination for which they are intended. Coin is fixed capital for a whole country, just as a railroad; for the manufacturer it is circulating capital. Wages to the master who pays them are circulating capital, to the workmen to whom they are paid they are merely incomings.

In each kind of industry a normal proportion exists between the two kinds of capital. A banker or a merchant possesses only circulating capital. On a railroad the capital is nearly all fixed.

It is unsafe for a manufacturer to have an insufficient floating capital, for this obliges him to depend largely on credit, which may be his ruin.

For a country it is unsafe to increase too rapidly the amount of fixed capital. If this be done there results a crisis such as that of 1847 in Europe, and those of 1856 and 1873 in America, all of which arose from the construction of too many railways.

J. S. Mill was inaccurate in his assertion, "industry is limited by capital." On the contrary, certain inventions, and even certain combinations, have the effect of greatly increasing the power of industry by diminishing the amount of capital it need employ. Thus, as we have seen, the division of labour permits a great economy of implements. A steam engine, again, for navigation, while obtaining the same motive power, costs and burns much less than thirty years ago. It is especially by the more scientific employment of the forces of nature that the power of industry has been increased.

Capital by immobilising the labour of to-day saves that of to-morrow. In primitive times a Rebecca goes to the well to fetch water which she carries in a pitcher on her head. Here the pitcher is the only capital employed, but the journey to and fro consumes much time. Later on, a well is dug and a pump built. The capital sunk is greater, but the daily labour much less. At last, and at considerable cost, waterworks are constructed. The capital employed in making the conduits, &c., is now ten or twenty times greater; but a tap has only to be turned, and more water is procured than Rebecca could have fetched if she had run about all day.

§ 2. The Formation of Capital.

Capital is the offspring of saving. If the means of subsistence for three days are procured by the labour of one, and the two days of leisure are employed in making a spade, with which more produce can be obtained from the earth and in less time, the amount of spare time will be further increased, and it will be more easy to construct fresh implements. Every step in advance renders it easier to make still greater strides. This example supplies a key to all the mysteries of the creation of capital. For the spade to be made, the previous labour must have left a surplus, which is the net produce, and for this surplus to be employed, not in idle enjoyment, but in the construction of a useful implement, the labourer must possess the virtue of prudence to induce him to sacrifice a present enjoyment to a future gain.

To put by wealth for the future constitutes saving, but to consume this wealth in making an article which will enable future commodities to be produced with less exertion is the best form which saving can take. To save by creating capital is thus no mere abstention from consumption, it is consumption so regulated as to give birth to an instrument which will increase production, and consequently consumption also. During the two days devoted to making the spade sustenance is consumed. If the time had been passed in amusement, exactly the same amount would have been consumed. The difference is that the saver, thanks to his spade, is better off for the future, while the spendthrift must continue to scratch the earth with his hands. The error is thus manifest of those who believe that the saving which creates capital is a check on the consumption and circulation of wealth, or, in the popular phrase, is "bad for trade."

The crowd curses the avaricious miser and praises the spendthrift with its usual folly. Miser and spendthrift are alike foolish, but the first only wrongs himself, the second harms others also.

The creation of capital by saving will increase with every increase of the productiveness of labour and of men's inclination to thrift. Where a day's labour produces a bare day's sustenance, the creation of capital by saving is an impossibility. As soon, however, as labour becomes more productive so that one day's work produces enough sustenance for three, there is a net produce available of food for two days. This food can be made the means of producing instruments of labour, and it will be used for this purpose if the owner of it is disposed to save. This disposition is the result of habits acquired in childhood, at school for instance, of the customs of the country, of public opinion, of the safety and facility of investment, and lastly of the profits which investments can return.

Saving is permanent and really useful to society only when it results in the creation of fresh capital.

The greater the destitution of an individual or country, the greater are .at once the necessity and the difficulty of saving. Hence the obstacles a poor nation has to encounter in escaping from its destitution. On the other hand, the possession of a capital to begin with, by increasing the productiveness of labour, facilitates the acquisition of fresh capital. Hence the increase of national wealth advances at an accelerating speed, and "to him who hath, more is given."

It is the spirit of economy shown in the creation of capital which has successively raised Holland, England, and the United States to power. It is an ignorant prodigality, shown in the destruction of capital, which completed the ruin of Spain from the time of Philip II. to the end of the last century.

§ 3. Tools and Machinery.

Among the objects which constitute capital it is especially tools and machines that render labour productive. Aristotle speaks of man as a "political animal," *i.e.* as suited for a social life. Adam Smith remarked that "man is the only animal that makes exchanges." Franklin speaks of him as "a tool-making animal." Thus it is from association, from exchange, and from tools that mankind derives its power over nature, or, in other words, its welfare and civilisation.

Everything over and above man's teeth and nails,

that assists labour, is a tool. A machine is a tool,
only it is a tool set in motion, no longer by human
muscles, but by the forces of nature, by a " motor."
Thus, as has been shown, the history of the
progress of tools is the history of the progress
of civilisation.

Industry has had recourse to motors of ever
increasing power, and ever better adapted to its
needs, first to the domesticated animals, then to
water, then to wind, then to steam, then to
electricity, which last is as yet in its infancy.

The advantages of machines are many and
great. They may be briefly enumerated as
follows :—

(i.) They bring into man's service forces of almost
limitless extent. It is reckoned that the power of
the machinery worked by steam in the civilised
countries is equivalent to that of fourteen million
horses, or of more than two hundred and eighty
million slaves. Besides this there are in the world
locomotives with a total power of twenty million
horses, and steam vessels of another four million.
The horse power of these calculations is equal to
that of at least two real horses, and thus we have
an equivalent for forty-eight million horses working
at the transport of men and their goods. In fixed
machinery, France possesses three million horse
power, and Belgium half a million. Reckoning
this unit of horse power as equal to the power of
twenty-one men, we find that to each French and

Belgian family there are five iron slaves, always ready, never tired, and amply nourished by a small supply of coal.

In ancient times, slaves, as we may read in the *Odyssey*, used to crush corn by hand in stone mortars. Later on, like Plautus, they were set to turn a mill. Towards the end of the Roman Republic there was introduced from Asia the water-mill. Antiparos, a Greek poet, celebrates as follows this labour of nature in the service of man, the marvel from which has issued every improvement in production. "Slaves who turn the mill, spare your toil and sleep in peace. It is to no purpose that the cock's shrill tones herald the dawn; take ye your sleep. By command of Ceres, the task of the young maidens is performed by Naiads, and these are now bounding in all their agile brilliancy upon the turning wheel. Let us live the happy life of our fathers, and enjoy at our ease the bounty which the goddess showers upon us." Machinery thus creates either leisure, or, if the will exists to employ this leisure in further production, additional wealth.

(ii.) Thanks to these mighty forces, men now execute enormous works which are the wonders of our time—the tunnels of Mont Cenis and the Saint Gothard, and those that are in progress under the Simplon and the Pyrenees; canals across the isthmuses of Suez and Panama which change the constitution of continents and the highways of commerce ; the draining of the lake of Harlem, working of mines at three and four thousand feet below sea level, a telegraph that encircles the entire globe with a network of wire along which human thoughts circulate with the swiftness of lightning.

(iii.) Machinery releases man from mechanical labour.   With the foresight usual to genius, Aristotle wrote, "If a tool could anticipate and execute the workman's orders, if the shuttle could transverse the woof of its own accord, art would have no more need of labourers, or masters of slaves."

(iv.) Machinery multiplies, sometimes enormously, the amount of produce which a given number of workmen can turn.out.   In cotton-spinning a single workman in charge of five hundred spindles does the work of a thousand spinners by hand.   In the same way, a knitting machine in a given time makes six thousand times as many stitches as a good work-woman.

(v.) The rapidity with which work is done spares manual labour, and, as a result, cheapens the price of all machine-made articles.   Lucifer matches can thus be sold at a penny the box of over a hundred, and a number of the *New York Herald*, containing as much matter as two volumes of 500 pages, 8vo, for five cents, or about twopence-halfpenny.

(vi.) Machinery does its work with perfect regularity and mathematical precision, witness its division of a metre into thousandth parts.

(vii.) Machinery makes the best use of raw

materials; thus a steam saw can cut up the thinnest planks.

(viii.) Machinery brings within a workman's means a whole host of useful and agreeable articles, once the exclusive property of the rich; for instance, printed cottons, which are no longer luxuries.

(ix.) The tendency of machinery is thus to promote equality among men, and it is consequently the cause and the ally of all democratic progress. Books and travelling are nowadays accessible to all.

Certain kinds of machinery are open to the reproach of sometimes imposing on workmen labours which exhaust and emaciate them, or give rise to special diseases. On the other hand, however, the old low, ill-ventilated rooms are now replaced by large workshops, in which the rules of hygiene are usually observed. It is the duty of employers, and failing these, of the state, to obviate the evils which may sometimes accompany the use of machinery. The science which invents the machines, provides the means for their safe employment.

§ 4. Does Machinery diminish the Employment and Wages of Workmen ?

This is the present state of affairs in Europe. The country in which industry employs most machines is England, and England is also the country in, which industry employs most workmen. The country in which industry employs fewest machines is

Russia, and Russia is also the country in which industry employs fewest workmen. Thus, far from diminishing employment, machinery actually increases the number of workmen. The explanation of this may be stated as follows.

A great proprietor maintains on his estate a hundred workmen who labour for him. He invents sundry machines, which enable him to save one-half of the manual labour, so that for the future fifty men are sufficient to do all his work. Will he then leave the other fifty, whose labour is no longer necessary, unemployed, and cast into the sea, as useless, the food with which they were nourished? Certainly not. He will continue to support them, and will employ them to do him fresh services. The same number of workmen will be employed, but more commodities will be produced, and more wants satisfied.

Take another case : the proprietor may content himself with the old amount of produce, and reduce by a half the number of hours he requires his hundred retainers to work. If he does this, the machines will have created additional leisure, instead of additional products. If all his rational wants were already satisfied, the second course will be the wiser; if this was not so, it is the first that will prevail. A country, viewed as one great consumer, is in exactly the position of this proprietor.

What happens is really this. Machinery shortens labour, and saves hand-work. The economy of hand-work lowers the prices of all fabrics, and with the

fall in price of these articles, the consumers have
money available, with which they purchase other
commodities. Workmen, whom the new machinery
has temporarily thrown out of employment, are again
taken on to make the articles which are the objects
of the new demand. Since the employment of workmen remains the same, while the means of subsistence does not diminish, there will be no reduction of
wages. On the contrary, the working classes will be
benefited, since with the same wages they will be
able to purchase a greater amount of the commodities whose prices have been lowered by the
use of machinery.

§ 5. How Machinery may compel Workmen to change their Occupation.

If consumers employ the money which machinery
enables them to save, in purchasing a greater amount
of the goods thus cheapened, all the workmen may
continue to work at this industry, employed in
producing greater quantities to meet the increased
demand. In this case the only difference will be
that wants will be more largely satisfied.

If, however, the consumers prefer to purchase new
products, workmen will be obliged to take to new
industries. Often they will only be able to do this
slowly and with difficulty; sometimes they will be
unable to do it at all, will suffer, perhaps even
succumb. They will have to endure a crisis. This
crisis will be of greater severity, if the new industry

is situated in another province, and worse still if it is transferred to another country. As soon, however, as it is passed, the same number of workmen will be employed, only there will have been a displacement which will leave more workmen in one place and fewer in another. A crisis of this sort was suffered in Flanders, when spinning machines broke the spindle in the hands of the country spinning women, and summoned a new class of workwomen to the factories at Ghent.

In these instances, happily of rare occurrence, it is the duty of employers of labour and of public bodies to come to the aid of the dispossessed workmen by instructing them, by facilitating their migration, and even by giving them actual help, as was done in Flanders in 1847. The new machinery benefits society at large, it is, therefore, intolerable that the workman, who is not responsible for the modifications introduced into industry, should be made their victim. Since he is deprived of his livelihood in the interests of the public good, he has a right, should he need it, to an indemnity, and the machinery which has increased production, affords the means of paying it.

§ 6. How Machinery increases the Employment of Workmen.

Thanks to machinery, the earth produces more new sources of wealth are being discovered, and works are multiplying on every side. In this way more workmen are employed, and at the same time there are more commodities to satisfy their hunger, their need of clothing, and their other wants. The number is incalculable of the workmen employed in industries which machinery has created, such as railroads, post offices, telegraphs, steamships, mines, great manufactories, and the construction of machines themselves. Printing employs twenty times more workmen than there were ever copyists transcribing manuscripts. Transport, again, demands the services of a hundred times the number of people it used to employ when people and produce grew up side by side.

J. S. Mill has remarked with profound sadness, that it is doubtful if hitherto all the machines that have been invented have decreased the sum of human labour by a single hour. Far from the hours of labour being decreased, far more men work at present and work for a longer time. Formerly the night brought sleep to all, and the Sabbath, rest. Now numbers are kept at work all night, on railroads, on ships, in the depths of coal mines, in blast furnaces, in sugar refineries, at offices, and even in the laboratory or library of the student, everywhere in fact where industrial process may not be interrupted, and the activity of modern life forbids delay. Man is harassed and consumed by these indefatigable iron slaves which he commands, but which he has also to serve, and whose activity "doth make the night joint-labourer to the day."

H

The immediate remedy for this excess of toil is to preserve with all possible scrupulousness, at least one day out of the seven to be spent in complete rest by those who are incessantly occupied with daily toil. Hereafter, when all rational wants are satisfied, machines will be required to cease the incessant increase of productions, and create more leisure for that true life, which, as the Greeks so well understood, is the life of the soul.

CHAPTER VI.

THE ESTABLISHMENT OF AN EQUILIBRIUM BETWEEN PRODUCTION AND CONSUMPTION.

WHEN so many and such powerful machines are seen at work on every side, the question arises as to how this enormous and ever-increasing quantity of products will find purchasers and consumers. Will not the lack of an outlet some day produce a glut ?

Economists reply that a general glut is impossible, since it is a fundamental principle that "products exchange for products," and thus if everybody who may wish to exchange offers twice as much as heretofore, the exchange will be effected exactly the same, the equation will be maintained, and the sole difference will be that every one will give and receive twice as much. A partial glut, however, is perfectly possible, if some one industry greatly increases its production while its customers have neither the wish nor the means to buy the surplus thus created. In the first of the cases they contemplate, economists have made an unfair use of mathematical formulas. Even if we suppose a general and identical increase of production a glut might arise, since the consumption of the various commodities could not possibly increase at a uniform rate. If twice the number of hats were made it is very unlikely that they would all be sold.

The true answer to our problem is that when there is a lack of equilibrium between production and consumption certain influences come into play which tend to restore this in the following way.

First Case.—Too few shoes are made. Those desirous of them will bid against each other for their possession. The price will rise, and shoemakers, gaining a greater profit, will make a greater number of shoes till the equilibrium is established.

Second Case.—Too many shoes are made. To sell the surplus shoemakers will lower their prices. This will have two results : first, the fall of prices will increase the number of consumers ; secondly, shoemakers, finding themselves at a loss, will make fewer shoes, until the equilibrium is here again established.

In this way, by the fluctuation between the rise and fall of prices a certain equilibrium, though always an unstable one, tends to be established

H 2

about the point at which production satisfies consumption.

CHAPTER VII.

CLASSIFICATION OF USEFUL OCCUPATIONS.

THE time-honoured classification of the different branches of production, and the one usually illustrated in sculpture and painting on public monuments, is that which distinguishes them into agriculture, manufacture, and commerce.

In international exhibitions the order followed is often that of the completion of the products and according to the wants which these supply. Raw materials and articles of food, building, furniture, clothing, artistic manufactures, and the fine arts.

The following is an expansion of a classification based on the actual nature of the labour, proposed by M. Dunoyer. This distinguishes—

I. Labours which have to do with men, and consist in the rendering of services.

II. Labours which have to do with things, and produce material commodities.

These may be subdivided into—

(i.) *Extractive* industries, which demand from nature useful substances without either modifying these or preserving the sources from which they are obtained. Such are the gathering of wild fruits, fishing, hunting, and the working of virgin forests, mines and quarries.

(ii.) *Agriculture,* which also extracts commodities from the soil, but preserves in good condition the sources of their production ; and above all sets in motion the organic force called life, which multiplies both vegetation and animals.

(iii.) *Manufactures,* which receive the materials obtained by the two preceding kinds of labour, and by the help of physical and chemical forces so fashion them that the made-up articles are able to satisfy the different human wants. Thus out of wool is made cloth, and out of flax, linen.

(iv.) *Commerce,* which summons goods to where they are wanted, and preserves, unites, and divides them to suit the convenience of consumers.

(v.) *Transport,* which conveys men and articles to the places where they are of the greatest use.

CHAPTER VIII.

OCCUPATIONS WHICH HAVE TO DO WITH MEN.

IT has been maintained that such occupations as those of the physician or the magistrate, although useful and even necessary, are not productive, since they do not produce any of those material objects with which political economy is alone concerned. A more careful analysis would have made it plain that any useful labour is necessarily productive, since in this case the two adjectives have nearly the same meaning. Those who render services to their fellows by procuring them greater security, health, or instruction, ought to be regarded as the partners of the labourers who work upon material objects. In the social workshop they are indirect producers, and we have here an application of the division of labour.

If a farmer could not rely on the services of the policeman, the magistrate and the schoolmaster, he would have to spend his time in teaching his children, guarding his stacks, and judging crimes and suits. Thanks to the help of the members of special professions he is able to devote all his time to his farm. In this way more products are obtained, and every article is better made.

Once more, the labours which aim at giving society security, justice, health, and instruction are by far the most productive of any, since without these the work of production languishes or dies outright. Capital is secreted or never amassed, manufacture dares not spread its wings, credit hardly exists, commerce is timid, or a nonentity. Of all this the East furnishes an example.

CHAPTER IX.

OCCUPATIONS CONCERNED WITH THINGS.

§ 1. Extractive Industries.

IN prehistoric times, as among the populations which still remain in savagery, the gathering wild fruits, fishing, and the chase supply man with all he consumes, the food he eats, and the skins with which he is clothed. In the Europe of to-day gathering wild fruits is little more than a memorial of the golden age, and hunting a pleasure which costs more than it returns. Only fishing has preserved any importance. This still everywhere furnishes a notable amount of a light and nutritious food. In Norway it is estimated to produce as much as agriculture. Moreover, it has played a great part in history by furnishing ships of war with their best sailors, a service which in some countries has rendered it the object of sometimes undue encouragement. The process of barrelling herrings, invented by Willem Benkels, of Biervliet, created the large fisheries of Holland, and these were the training school of those "sea-beggars" who beat the Spaniards, and of the fearless sailors who carried the flag of the Netherlands on every sea.

The working of mines in our own days has made an immense stride. Besides the precious metals the ancients extracted from the soil copper, tin, and iron, but all in small quantities. To-day the mining industry is the basis of every other, since it supplies the coal which has been well called "the bread of industries."

Iron, again, is of such importance that it is said that the material prosperity of a country may be measured by the amount of this metal which it consumes. The statistics of a single one of its branches will suffice to give an idea of the present importance of the mining industry. In 1880 there were produced three hundred and forty-three million tons of coal, the value of which, at the very low price of eight shillings a ton, would be 137,200,000*l.*

All the extractive industries have the unfortunate characteristic of exhausting the sources of their production, which they are powerless either to create or in any sensible degree reconstitute. Pisciculture may transform fishing into an "agriculture of the rivers and sea," and on this account deserves the utmost consideration, both of the State and of individuals.

But what are men to do when they once have burnt the layers of combustible matter which represent the accumulated forests of the geological eras and the warmth of the sun stored in the secondary strata ? It is calculated that in Europe there is coal enough to last for three or four centuries, but scarcity will make itself felt long before the complete exhaustion of the supply. Already in many countries iron, lead, zinc, and copper are becoming rare. Every store that cannot be renewed must end by being exhausted.

To whom, in the interests of production, should mines belong? In England they are the property of the owners of the surface. In France and Belgium by the law of 1810 they are assigned to the State, which concedes the right of working them to individuals, reserving to itself a rent and general supervision. The French system appears the better of the two, since it avoids subdivision, and allows of concessions being granted such extension as may be most adapted to a wise system of working.

§ 2. Agriculture.

The ancients held, and rightly, that no other labour is at once as good for mind and body, and so worthy of a free man as agriculture. In the fine words of Cicero : " *Omnium rerum ex quibus aliquid acquiritur, nihil est agricultura melius : nihil uberius, nihil dulcius, nihil homine libero dignius* (*De Officiis*, i. 42). Elsewhere he again remarks that the pleasures of those who till the soil are almost as elevated as those of the philosophic life. *Voluptates agricolarum mihi ad sapientis vitam proxime videntur accedere.* Cato the Elder pronounces this fine eulogy on agriculture : *Pius quæstus, stabilissimus, minimeque invidiosus. Minimeque male cogitantes sunt qui in eo studio occupati sunt* (*Cato Major*, 15, § 51). " Holy calling, most steadfast and most free from envy : they who engage in this pursuit have their thoughts least set on evil." Xenophon in the *Country Economy* of Ischomachos paints the life of a Greek farmer in all its happiness and social usefulness. Horace is never tired of vaunting the felicity of the country life: *Beatus ille qui . . . paterna rura bobus exercet suis, solutus omni fœnore* (Epode ii). The type of those brave peasants who used the same hand to guide the plough and wield the spear, like Cincinnatus, was always admired by the Romans, especially in the days of the decline.

At the present time attention and encouragement are exclusively given to the manufacturing industries. This is a mistake. If it be more important to make men healthy and happy, than to incessantly increase production, it is agriculture that deserves every advantage. Sully's saying will always be right: "Tillage and pasturage are the two breasts of the State."

Quesnay and his disciples, who, from their desire to regulate societies by the order of nature, were called *physiocrates*, maintained that the labour of the farmer is the only one which leaves a surplus on which the other professions can live. On the other hand, Destutt de Tracy asserts that a farm is only a factory like any other.

As to the essence of the matter in dispute, the physiocrates were in the right. Undoubtedly, despite their arguments, the other industries are productive, since they increase the utility of things by rendering

them fit for our use ; but the farmer sets at work
not only physical and chemical but also vital forces,
and thus multiplies commodities. He sows one
grain of corn and reaps twenty ; this year he has a
couple of sheep, in a few years he will have a flock.
Agriculture is the first of industries, because it is
the foundation of all the others. These can only
increase the number of persons they employ, if the
farms supply them with more food.

Real civilisation dates from the day when man
first intrusted a grain of corn to the soil; from that
day forward it has been his interest to live at peace
with his fellows. So long as he was supported by
the chase or even by cattle-farming, disputes might
arise as to the run of the game or the pastures of
the flocks. It was at this time that Hobbe's atrocious
phrase, *Homo homini lupus,* man a wolf to his fellow,
was really true. As soon as he drew his subsistence
from the soil, a subsistence extracted by the sweat of
his brow, man was forced to desire that justice should
take the place of violence, in order that he might
gather in security the fruits of his toil.

§ 3. The Progress of Agriculture.

The domestication of animals preceded agriculture,
and was a great step in the progress of primitive
man, whose meal no longer depended on a chance
javelin shot, but was always ready at hand. The
pastoral system has lasted unaltered in certain
countries adapted to it, such as Arabia and Tartary.

It is still the most advantageous in countries where
at the outset population is scarce and pasture lands
extensive, as in Australia, Natal, and the pampas of
La Plata.

Agricultural progress has consisted in obtaining
from the same space a larger amount of produce by
the employment of better processes and larger
capital. From being *extensive* cultivation has
become *intensive*. This truth has been well expressed by Palladius, a Latin agriculturist of the
fourth century, who summed up the works of his
three illustrious predecessors, Cato, Varro, and
Columella. His words are : *Fecundior est culta exi-
guitas quam magnitudo neglecta.* "A little field well
tilled is more productive than a large one neglected."

At the outset cultivation was intermittent and at
times even nomadic. The surface soil was burnt
and a crop obtained from the ashes ; eighteen or
twenty years had then to elapse for spontaneous
vegetation to restore to the soil its elements of
fertility.

At a later date, by the side of the large tracts
reserved as pastures, the arable land lies fallow every
other year in biennial rotation, or one year in three
in triennial. Still later, the earth is given no rest at
all, but by alternating cereals with fodder and roots
is made to yield a harvest every year. Finally, by
continually increasing the amount of manure, by the
system of "stolen crops," two harvests may be
obtained in a single year. Thus, the fundamental

principle of agriculture is to restore to the soil as
much as is taken from it, and even to add fresh
fertilizing matter such as lime, chalk, Peruvian
guano, phosphates, ditch mud, and the sewage of
towns. *Thievish* cultivation, *Raubcultur*, as the great
chemist Liebig well called it, sterilises the most
productive regions, such as those of Sicily and
Algeria, once the granaries of ancient Rome.

The forms of property have passed through a
similar development to those of cultivation. Originally collective and communal, it came, later on, to
belong to the family and finally to the individual.

In Belgium the different agricultural regions still
present a picture of the successive stages of agricultural progress, and the most primitive methods of
cultivation are to be found in the districts geologically
the most ancient and the most elevated. On the
plateau of the Ardennes, the first schists which
emerged from the primitive ocean, the collective
lands of the commune are prepared by fire, every
fifteen or twenty years to give a crop of rye. The soil
of Condroz, built upon limestone or on schists more
recent than those of the Ardennes, is cultivated by a
triennial rotation. The biennial system is dominant on
the clay of the herbage; finally, on the modern and
well cultivated sands of Flanders prevails the intensive system of high farming and double crops. Thus
in ascending, stage by stage, from the sea board to
Luxembourg the traveller ascends at once the scale
of altitudes, epochs of agriculture, and geological eras.

§ 4. Large and Small Farming.

It is often discussed whether preference should be given to large or small farming.   Large farming may be taken as cultivating an extent of more than a hundred acres, small farming as working less than twenty-five.

If it is above all things advantageous to a country to be inhabited by a vigorous race of proud and independent peasant proprietors, like that of Rome in the early days of the republic, or those of Switzerland, France, and Norway in our own times, small farming, united with peasant proprietorship, is far superior to large.   It may be added that, except in England, small farming everywhere yields a larger gross, and even a larger net product.   To be convinced of this it is only necessary to compare districts respectively of large and small farming in the different countries of Europe ; in Italy, the small *poderi* of Tuscany with the *latifundia* of the Roman States and Sicily ; in Spain, the bare plains of Castille with the neighbourhood of Barcelona or Valentia ; in Portugal, the desert wastes of Alementego with the smiling *aforamentos* of the northern provinces ; in France, the departments of the centre with those of the north ; in Prussia, the provinces of the East with those of the Rhine ; and in Belgium, Flanders with Condroz.

In England large farming and large properties have killed this class of free and brave peasant proprietors, the yeomen who won the battles of Poitiers, Crécy, and Agincourt. The following table shows how small is the rural population in England :—

DIVISION OF THE POPULATION AMONG THE
DIFFERENT OCCUPATIONS.

	Agriculture.	Manufactures.	Commerce.
England	26	43	15
France	53	26	11
Prussia	54	30	6
United States	48	21	9
Belgium	31	30	7

Never to be forgotten is Pliny's cry of grief which echoes like a warning voice through economic history: *Latifundia perdidere Italiam et provincias.* "Overgrown estates ruined Italy and the provinces." Large properties everywhere produce excessive inequality, depopulation, class divisions, and decay. Countries inhabited by peasant proprietors have withstood all these crises. The farmer who is his own landlord, who sees on his field the fruits of his toil, who pays neither rent nor wages, can brave without fear both foreign competition and the variations of prices.

§ 5. Manufacturing Industries.

The manufacturing industries receive from the extractive and agricultural their raw materials and give them the final form demanded by consumption In primitive times the labour of the manufacturer was closely connected with that of the husbandman. In the home of the Greek or Roman, who lived by the produce of their fields, the women spun the flax and made the clothes. The same organisation of labour is found on the estates of Charlemagne and at the present day there are examples of it in India, in Russia, and amongst the Slavs ot the Danube.

Whenever the ease of communication makes it possible, the division of labour calls into being the workmen with a special craft. Industry can then make a great advance, as has been seen in antiquity in Phœnicia and Egypt, and in the middle ages in the Italian republics, and the Flemish communes. It continues, however, to preserve its domestic character, and still remains manufacture on a small scale.

Manufacture on a large scale comes into being with mechanical motive powers. The contrast between these two forms of production is very striking. Even when the weavers of Bruges or Florence were sending their clothes to all the markets of Europe, the work was carried on by the domestic hearth, as one sees in the illustrations of manuscripts. The children cleaned the wool, the wife spun it, and the husband, helped by some journeymen, worked at the loom. The capital employed is small; the circle of workpeople limited. Equality prevails between the master-workman and the hands he employs; they have the same labours, the same kind of life and the same mental culture. The market for which they work is known and assured.

Nowadays a large capital unites in a large work-shop, around the engine which supplies the power, a perfect crowd of workmen, separated from their hearths, and working for a market which sometimes expands and sometimes contracts or closes. The head of this army of industry is wealthy or largely paid, for his position demands varied and unusual aptitudes, the power of governing, technical know-ledge, an acquaintance with the markets, the spirit of order in administration, and, above all, good sense in business matters. Ways of life and mental culti-vation have thus opened a great gulf between the employers who furnish the capital and the labourers who lend their strength. Hence results what is called "the conflict of labour and capital," and all the novel phenomena of the existing economic order.

Even in the manufacturing countries of the West, industries on a small scale employ more workmen than those on a large. For instance, in France, at the census of 1872, there were reckoned to be 950,000 men employed in the first as against 909,000 in the second. It is plain, however, that manufacture on a large scale is everywhere gaining ground. It is even invading what might have seemed the special field of bespoken labour, the making of clothes and shoes. This is explained by the advantages it possesses, which are as follows:

I

(1) Application on a large scale of the principle of the division of labour. Over each duty is set a man specially suited for it ; thus, on a great railroad there will be "specialties" for the maintenance of the line, for the rolling-stock, for the traction, for the combustibles, for the tariffs, for the commercial details, and for litigation.

(2) Relative diminution of the general expenses. Among the expenses of production there are some which arise from the very nature of the enterprise, and, like patent fees, scarcely vary ; others, again, vary in proportion to the activity of production, like the fuel in a steam engine. The first expenses are called "general, or fixed," the second "variable, or proportional." From this very definition it follows that the first expenses must become relatively smaller with every increase in the total produced by the enterprise.

(3) Less capital is required to create the same produce. A furnace casting ten thousand tons of iron a year will cost less than two furnaces each casting five thousand.

(4) Employment of machines of exceptional power, sometimes carrying with them a monopoly, like the famous Krupp hammer, which cost 200,000*l.*

(5) Purchase of raw material on a large scale and consequently at cheaper prices, and a greater profit made on waste.

(6) Greater means for finding markets, agencies, foreign travellers, world-wide reputation, &c.

(7) Coalitions effecting economies, as does an amalgamation of the systems of different railways.

(8) The expenses of the original model reduced with every increase of production ; for example, where 50,000 copies of a paper are printed the cost per copy of setting up the type becomes insignificant.

The inconveniences of industry on a large scale are as follows :—

(1) It removes the workman from his family life. This evil is aggravated when wives also are employed.

(2) It diminishes the power of personal interest and the efficaciousness of what is called " the master's eye."

(3) By working for an unknown and very variable market it is exposed to frequent crises.

(4) It crowds workmen together in certain localities which are thus made unhealthy. This last defect, however, can be obviated by building workmen's houses.

§ 6. Necessary Conditions of Industries on a large Scale.

Industry on a large scale can only be developed when certain conditions occur together.

(1) Cheap means of transport—the sea, canals, or railroads—to bring vast amounts of raw materials and carry away vast amounts of fabrics.

(2) A good political, civil, and judicial organisation,

assuring the security necessary to the employment of large capitals.

(3) A capable staff, especially for the management, as the success of an enterprise mainly depends on the skill of its directors.

It is often strangers who introduce a new industry into a country ; thus the first railroads were almost everywhere constructed by Englishmen. These foreigners should not be regarded with jealousy ; they come to open up fresh sources of wealth. The first care, however, of a government should be to create institutions that will serve as training schools for good industrial managers.

§ 7. Industries of Transport.

Industries of transport contribute to the production of wealth by carrying articles to the places where they are most wanted and will be proportionately most useful. Transport is thus the ally and instrument of commerce. Sometimes it even creates the whole value of certain products which, useless in one place, so soon as they are conveyed elsewhere acquire great utility. Transport in this acts in the same way as the extractive industries which obtain minerals from the bosom of the earth in which they were lying useless. Again, by conveying men and commodities transport disseminates the benefits of new discoveries, multiplies the relations between nations, indistinguishably intertwines their interests, softens or destroys their antipathies, and finally makes their fraternity and co-operation something more than a word or a dream. It is thus a powerful agent of civilisation throughout the whole world.

The progress made in the means of transport is truly astonishing. A horse can carry on his back and on a footpath 2 cwt. at most; in a cart and on a macadamized road 2 tons; on the rails of a tramway 10 tons; on a canal or by sea 100 tons; lastly, by river, that walking road, as Pascal calls it, the bulk of the burden makes no difference, as is seen in the case of the huge timber rafts.

The Romans were the first who knew how to construct the splendid roads, whose huge polygonal slabs resting on a foundation of mortar, may still be seen in the neighbourhood of Rome. These strategic roads, linking the most distant provinces with the centre of the Empire, served also the ends of commerce, and caused Roman civilisation to penetrate everywhere.

The advantages of improved channels of communication are numerous.

(1) By diminishing the expenses of transport they enable goods to be sold to producers at higher profits, and at the same time allow of these buying more cheaply what they have to procure for their manufactures. As a result there is an increase in the value of the sources of production, lands, forests, mines, and quarries, and an immense aggrandisement of the national wealth.

(2) Merchandise is sent to market in greater quantities and, consequently, consumers obtain it at cheaper rates.

(3) Rise of prices at the place of output; fall of prices at the place of consumption; tendency of prices towards uniformity.

(4) Aggrandisement of the large towns, especially capitals. The attraction which these exercise on the seekers after employment, instruction, pleasure, seclusion or society, is no longer counterbalanced by the dearness of living. When, however, this aggrandisement of cities is favoured by an excess of political and administrative centralization it becomes a great evil.

§ 8. Should Roads be made, and Means of Transport provided from Public Funds ?

Should the State, the county, the union, construct highways, ports, canals, and railroads ? If individuals undertake these tasks, so much the better; if not, it lies with the public authorities to take action; and for two reasons. In the first place, after public instruction there is no more powerful cause of progress than an improvement in the means of communication. In the second, since the nation profits by any increase in the revenue of taxes, or in the value of all the sources of production, it follows that the construction of railroads, &c., even though they yield no direct profit, is yet a most advantageous investment of the public funds. This can

be shown by keeping a strict account of debit and
credit. To debit put down the cost of construction,
to credit the increased value of lands, forests, mines,
and quarries, the new industries which spring up,
and the improvements in agriculture; the credit side
of the account will be by far the larger.

The much discussed question as to whether the
State ought also to take upon itself the working of
railways is of the most complex character. Perhaps
it should be answered by the economist in the
affirmative, by the politician in the negative. Possibly both parties might be satisfied if all the lines
were concentrated in the hands of the State, which
should then entrust their working to a company
acting under Government control.

§ 9. Commerce.

In the clear and simple manner taught him by
Socrates, Xenophon explains the cause and the
advantages of commerce. "No town," he says,
"possesses at the same time both wood and flax, for
wherever flax is plentiful the country is flat and
without wood. One country has one commodity,
another another. It follows that every state is
obliged both to export and import. Commerce thus
enriches the city by substituting useful commodities
for articles which, by their excessive abundance, had
lost all value."

In the words of Montesquieu—"The natural effect
of commerce is a tendency towards peace." How,

indeed, is it possible to inflict harm upon an enemy without either ruining a debtor or killing a customer? Commerce, again, applies between nation and nation the fertile principle of the division of labour. This is admirably expressed in a sentence of President Garfield—" Commerce makes all mankind a family of brothers, in which the welfare of each member depends on that of the others. It thus creates that unity of our race which causes the resources of the whole world to be at the disposal of each individual."

The maxim of commerce is to buy cheap and sell dear. Stimulated by self-interest, the merchant is ceaselessly summoning commodities from where they are over abundant and consequently cheap, to sell them where they are scarce and therefore dear; and in doing this he is serving the general interest. Retail traders choose goods with discrimination, buy them under the best conditions, class them in assortments, preserve and sell them in small quantities in such a way as to suit the resources and needs of the consumers. Were it possible to abolish these middlemen and bring customers face to face with producers, nothing could be better. Meanwhile, however, the middlemen render very real services

CHAPTER X.

COLONIES.

IN speaking of commerce, a few words must be said on the subject of colonies, since it is imagined nowadays, very wrongly, that a state must have colonies if it is to have a flourishing trade and large navy.

The commercial city of Tyre and, later on, Carthage, established factories for trading purposes, and these developed into colonies and flourishing towns. The Greek cities founded colonies as outlets for the surplus population deprived by the slaves of the resource of manual labour. Despite the diminishing population of Italy, Rome founded colonies by establishing veteran soldiers and the poorer burgesses on lands wrested from the conquered nations. The object was to "romanise" the provinces and consolidate the imperial rule, and it was completely attained. In modern times the Spaniards and Portuguese founded colonies as a means of obtaining what was believed to be the most real kind of wealth, the precious metals. The Dutch and English afterwards followed their example in order to develop their trade and gain a monopoly of the sale of certain products much sought after in Europe.

Little by little from out a mass of restrictive regulations was born the " colonial system." This system rested on two monopolies. The mother country reserved to itself the exclusive right of purchasing the products of the colonies and selling them in Europe. It thus reckoned, in the absence of all competition, to buy cheaply and sell dear. This was the first monopoly. Again, it reserved to itself the exclusive right of selling in the colonies its made up goods, once more reckoning, in the absence of competition, to obtain extremely high prices. This was the second monopoly. Both hopes were deceived, and the violation of freedom produced, as usual nothing but bitter fruits. On the one side, the colonies, crushed beneath so many obstacles, continued poor and purchased little; on the other the inhabitants of the parent country paid high prices for the products of their colonies, which free trade would have brought to them at cheaper rates. Their slender profits were thus more than counterbalanced by the disguised tax they had imposed on themselves. To this must be added the cruel working of the Indians, the slavery of the blacks, the frightful amount of blood and money which their enfranchisement has cost in the colonies of England, France, and recently of the United States, the destruction of the ancient civilisations of Mexico and Peru, the ruinous cost of maintaining armies and fleets, and, lastly, half a century of barbarous wars between European states rising out of colonial relations. If all these be taken into consideration the total loss will far outweigh the total profit.

Undoubtedly the discovery of America and the trade with Asia have enlarged the dominion of the human race, and procured it the enjoyment of a large number of useful and agreeable products. But trade would have supplied the world with the same goods without making it pay so cruel a price. There is not a colony to-day which does not cost the inhabitants of the mother country more than it brings in.

No more magnificent possession can be imagined than India. An immense empire, peopled by 300,000,000 laborious and submissive inhabitants, and on the plains which descend in a gentle slope from the heights of the Himalayas to the sea, yielding every kind of product, because every kind of soil and climate is successively represented; an empire, again, which is the theatre of one of the most ancient civilisations of the world! Yet, if we look at its balance sheet, we find a permanent annual deficit, continual disquietudes, and, what is worse, smouldering jealousy or expensive wars with one or another of the European states; lastly, the whole foreign policy dominated by a single interest. The English economists have adjusted the balance, and it does not incline in their favour. The younger sons of well-to-do families are employed by the Indian treasury, but, in reality, it is the English people that pays them. The imperial crown which the Queen has recently placed on her forehead, has cost, and will cost again, **many a million of** her subjects' money.

For modern states the possession of colonies is an anachronism.   That it is so may be easily proved against objectors as follows :—

At the present day there are three kinds of colonies.   The first, countries in which the emigrants from the parent state can live, work, and beget children, as Australia, Canada, and South Africa. The second are military and victualling stations, such as Gibraltar, Malta, Aden, Singapore, Hong- kong.   The last are tropical regions, inhabited by races adapted to the climate, such as India and Java. Of these three kinds only the third need be con- sidered, because the first will soon emancipate them- selves like the New England, which has now developed into the United States ; the second are only powerful fortresses scattered over the surface of the oceans for the protection of trade.

To govern colonies there is needed that spirit of continuity and authority which may be expected from an absolute power, but not from parliamentary ministers, who change at each election, and bring to the task of government views different if not opposed.   A parliament elected to regulate the affairs of the mother country has neither inclination nor capacity to concern itself with those of the colonies.   In England, when the Indian budget is discussed in Parliament, hardly fifty members stay in the House.   Again, colonial affairs become com- plicated with those of the home country—themselves sufficiently intricate — and   still   further   increase the difficulties and instability of parliamentary government. An example of this may be found in Holland.

White men, who cannot work under a tropical sun, live of necessity from the tax exacted on the labour of the old inhabitants. This system was formerly considered a natural one; to-day it is attacked by those who defend the rights of humanity, and cannot last much longer. As soon as the equality of the different races is accepted as a dogma, equal rights are demanded for the aborigines; but these rights cannot be granted while the aborigines are kept in a state of subjection.

What an impulse would be given to education and every kind of civilisation if to their promotion were devoted the money devoured in maintaining the military and naval forces and in the frontier wars occasioned by colonies.

The greatest evil of all is that the possession of colonies multiplies, between people and people, points of contact, and causes of dissension. To this the differences perpetually arising between England and the United States are a standing witness.

In the present state of the world peace is such an inestimable blessing that all the colonies together both past and present, are not worth a single year of war. England, the greatest colonial power that has ever existed, understands this. She cedes the Ionian Islands to Greece, and sets an example of prudence which cannot be too much admired. She

laments the acquisition of Cyprus; she counts the
cost of her possession of India; she is paving the
way for the complete emancipation of Australia,
Canada, and South Africa.   If a country has more
money than it knows what to do with it should
colonise its own waste lands: in France, Sologne; in
Italy, Calabria; in Belgium, Campine.   States
which have no colonies may console themselves, and
states which have colonies should prepare to lose
them, for in this loss they will find a gain.

CHAPTER XI.

ASSOCIATIONS FOR THE COMBINATION OF CAPITAL.

INDUSTRIES on a large scale need a large capital.
Who is to furnish it ?   Formerly the employer contributed all the capital necessary, which was either
wholly his own or borrowed on his credit.   To-day
this capital is usually formed by a combination of
the capitals of a large number of persons.   In this
way the risk is shared in fractions.   Each share-
holder only ventures a small part of his property, and
remembers the useful proverb: " All the eggs should
not be carried in the same basket."   The telegraph
cable across the Atlantic was estimated to cost
1,200,000*l*., and the experts asserted that the electric

spark could not traverse the ocean. Baron Roths-
child himself would not have ventured the whole
sum needed. But when the capital was divided, a
share of the risk was no longer appalling; millions
of persons subscribed for shares; the electric cable
was a success, and to-day links together all the
continents across the seas. In this way a financial
combination—the association of capitals—came to
the assistance of science and enabled it to realise
its wonders. Thanks to this principle of association,
isthmuses are cut, mountains pierced, and every
country in succession endowed with railroads,
factories, banks, and all the enterprises which aim
at turning the gifts of nature to advantage.

Associations of capitals have taken certain definite
forms: these are the commercial companies. Of these
the laws of civilised countries recognise five distinct
kinds:—

(1) *Companies Trading under a Common Name.*—
These rest on no legal fiction. The shareholders
have all a certain control over the management.
They divide the profits in proportion to their contributions, but are indefinitely liable for all debts.
This form of association is suitable only to enterprises which present few risks. It was already
known in Roman times; thus Livy relates that the
provisions for Scipio's army fighting against the
Carthaginians in Spain were supplied by a company. The jurist, Ulpian, again speaks of banking
companies (*societates argentariæ*).

(2) *Companies with Mixed Liability (sociétés en commandité).*—In these some of the shareholders (*les commandités*) are active partners and have unlimited liability, others (*les commanditaires*) are sleeping partners who supply capital, but only venture the amount of their shares so long as they refrain from any participation in the management. This kind of company, which is more frequent in France than in England, is very convenient for supplying a person of special aptitude—an inventor for instance —with the funds that are indispensable for profiting by his exceptional qualities or invention. It was first used in the middle ages in the Italian republics as a means of evading the canon law which forbade, under the name of usury, any fixed remuneration for a loan of money. The possessors of capital entrusted it to traders, and stipulated to receive a share of the profits in the place of a fixed rate of interest.

(3) *Joint Stock Companies.*—In these no one, not even the manager or director, is responsible for more than the amount of his share, on condition that the laws are respected. This kind of company resembles a republic. All its authorities emanate from the body of shareholders. These nominate at a general meeting the chief of the executive, or manager, and the senate, or board of directors.

Joint stock companies first arose in the Low Countries in the seventeenth century, when they were formed for the purpose of organising those powerful associations which engaged in distant trade.

(4.) *Companies with limited liability* resemble the preceding, with the exception that no previous authorisation is necessary for their constitution. It is sufficient to comply with the rules laid down by the law.

The contributions of the members in these different forms of association can be, and usually are, represented by documents called *bonds*.

(5.) *Co-operative societies* differ from others in the number of shareholders being variable, as also in the amount of their shares. They take as their aim the forming associations of workmen and artisans. The subscription, which is usually very small, can be paid in instalments to suit the convenience of small savers. The combination of these petty savings, which in isolation would have been powerless, constitutes a capital sufficiently large to obtain credit or to form the funds of an industrial enterprise.

The multiplication of joint stock companies is incredible. They are daily being started in every quarter and for every purpose. All new enterprises and most old ones are constituted in this form, and methods of possession have been really transformed. Of the causes of this astonishing success we have already indicated the first in the ease with which a great capital may be formed by the combination of small capitals and a division of risks. But, in the second place, joint stock companies obtain the most capable men to direct their affairs, and their managers, instead of being appointed by the chance of birth, are chosen by election from among the most capable administrators. Again, these companies give to industrial property that democratic form which our era demands. The manufacturing industries, as they develop, take the form of immense enterprises, which oust the smaller workshops and artisans from the market. Of themselves they thus tend to constitute a kind of industrial feudalism. But joint stock companies, by dividing and partitioning the proprietorship of large enterprises into a vast number of shares, each of a small amount, enable even working men to participate in their success. Since property is the necessary complement of freedom, the aim of civilisation should be to render the head of each household the proprietor of the instrument of his labour—the farmer of his field, the workman of his tool, or a share of the colossal machine into which the tool is often transformed. If a labourer purchase a share in the industrial company which employs him, the problem is at once solved; the conflict between labour and capital comes to an end.

By one of those frequent and natural harmonies between the changes introduced in the methods of production and the methods of possession, the joint stock company has become common at the moment of the development of industry on a large scale. It thus favours a subdivision of property increasingly democratic.

BOOK III.

DISTRIBUTION AND CIRCULATION.

PART I.—DISTRIBUTION.

CHAPTER I.

DISTRIBUTION : RENT, WAGES, INTEREST.

THREE factors contribute to the production of commodities—nature, labour and capital. Each must have a share of the product as its reward, and this share, if it is to be just, must be proportionate to the several contributions.

The share of the natural agents is Rent. The share of labour, Wages. The share of capital, Interest.

The clerk receives a salary; the lawyer and doctor, fees; the manufacturer, profits: salary, fees, and profits are so many forms of wages for services rendered.

K 2

As soon as the contributors have been rewarded with their several shares, they are able to make exchanges, and exchanges constitute the circulation of wealth. Distribution, therefore, precedes circulation.

CHAPTER II.

HOW DISTRIBUTION IS ACCOMPLISHED.

IN primitive societies such as existed before the rise of Rome, among the Italian tribes, and are still found in Norway and among the Slavs on the Danube, each father of a family cultivates his own patrimony, and produces all he consumes. Here there is no place for distribution ; labour, capital, and natural materials are all in the same hands. Remuneration is always fair. Each man gathers that which he sowed. Energy is rewarded, and indolence punished.

When, however, the three factors are in the hands of different persons, and, in consequence of the division of labour, each depends on a process of exchange for obtaining what he consumes, distribution is no longer an easy matter, and no longer in such strict proportion to the several contributions. It is now brought about by the agency of an " employer," who pays each "factor of production" just as much as competition forces him to give, retaining the surplus as his own profit.

Let us follow the fortunes of a loaf of bread. The farmer pays rent to his landlord, wages to his labourers, interest to the banker from whom he borrows; the surplus left when all payments have been made is his profit. The corn arrives at the miller's. He, in his turn, makes a similar distribution to reward the labour used in grinding it. The baker, who turns the flour into bread, does the same. Last of all, the consumer who buys the loaf pays a price sufficient to replace the advances which farmer, miller, and baker have successively made by way of rewarding the three factors.

Obviously, if the employer owns either the natural materials or the capital, he pays himself in the one case the rent, in the other the interest, or reckons it among his expenses.

CHAPTER III.

PRINCIPLES REGULATING DISTRIBUTION.

DISTRIBUTION is determined firstly by the civil institutions fixing the rights of individuals and the acquisition and inheritance of wealth; secondly, and subordinately to these, by authority, by custom, or by free contract regulated by competition.

The influence of the institutions of the state is plain. As in Egypt, the land, the great factories and, the railways may all belong to the sovereign. The soil of each parish may be owned in common by all the families of the village, as is the case in Great Russia. Again, as in France and Belgium, landed estates on the death of the proprietor may be equally divided among his children. In each of these cases, distribution will be very different from what it is in England, where landed property is held by a small number of rich proprietors, and descends, as a rule, to the eldest son.

Subserviently to the influence of institutions, the share of one or another of the factors of production may be regulated by custom, as in the case of the fees of the lawyer or physician ; by authority, as in that of the salary of civil servants ; or by contract and competition, as with wages and rent.

Formerly distribution was regulated, to a very considerable extent, by custom and authority. Thus in ancient Egypt and India, in the same way as in our own western countries during the middle ages, wages, payments in kind, and rentals were all fixed by use and tradition. The metayer system, which shares the produce equally between landlord and tenant, has not changed since the days of antiquity. On the other hand, in our own times, distribution is almost entirely governed by contract and competition.

CHAPTER IV.

REWARD OF THE NATURAL AGENTS.

§ 1. Rent.

IF I fish in a well-stocked lake, hunt in a forest where game abounds, or cultivate a fertile soil, I obtain enough to live on and something over. Nature lends me her aid; and the greater her fertility, the greater will be the surplus which my labour, if well directed, will leave me over and above my necessary expenses.

This surplus, due to the happy direction of my labour and the productiveness of the natural agents, is natural rent. Whether I am obliged to pay it to the proprietors of these agents depends not on nature, nor on my industry, but on social conditions. If the extent of fertile land is unlimited, as in new countries, I shall pay nothing for the possession of a holding, as I can have one almost for the asking. In this case, then, I shall keep the natural rent, or surplus of produce over cost of production, for myself. If, however, the natural agents are already appropriated, I shall have to give up all or part of this surplus to the landlord to gain the right to work his lands. The proportion I shall have to pay will depend on the competition among landless farmers, bidding against each other for the holdings from which to gain a livelihood. If these are few in number I shall have little to pay; if, on the contrary, there are more would-be farmers than farms, I shall be reduced to surrender all the produce, save what is absolutely needful for my maintenance.

Anything that produces useful commodities and is limited in quantity may yield a rent, just as well as arable land, a waterfall which turns a mill, a river or lake containing fish, a quarry or mine, building ground, or an exceptionally fine voice. The possession of these things constitutes a monopoly, and their owners can therefore exact a rent from those who wish to enjoy them.

Labour expended on good land is more productive than the same amount spent on bad. To obtain the right to cultivate good land it is, therefore, worth while to pay a sum equivalent to the advantage obtained by its greater fertility. The excess of the produce over the cost of production constitutes the natural rent. The portion of this excess which circumstances force the farmer to pay to the proprietor is the effective rent.

It is often said that rent arises from the difference of fertility in different soils. This difference, however, is the cause of the different rates of rent, not of rent itself. As a matter of fact, if all lands were of the same quality they might all pay a rent, so long as they yielded a surplus, and so long as there were no waste lands to be appropriated. In Egypt the whole soil formed by the muddy deposit of the Nile is of an almost uniform quality, yet it all yields a very high rent.

A good situation, such as one near a market, a river, a railroad or the sea, increases the utility of land, and has the same effect as fertility in giving rise to a rent. Land in the centre of a large town is often worth £100 the square yard, and is let at a proportionately high rate.

Rent obeys the law which regulates value. It depends on utility and scarceness. The rent which a property yields increases in proportion firstly to the usefulness, and secondly to the rarity of its products.

§ 2. Theory of Rent held by Ricardo and Mill.

Ricardo, a disciple of Adam Smith, formulated a theory of rent which bears his name. According to this theory the most fertile lands are the first cultivated, and as long as any of these are available, rent has no existence. But, in time, population increases and the free lands are all occupied; agricultural produce is in greater demand, and prices rise. This rise in prices makes it profitable to cultivate land of inferior quality. But in the land market, as in any other, articles of the same quality cannot sell for different prices, nor the same prices be obtained for articles of different quality. In this way the greater surplus which the better lands yield brings rent into existence.

If population and prices continue to increase, recourse must be had to land of the third quality, and the rents of the other lands again rise.

It follows that the rent of any given land is the difference which exists between the produce of this land and that of the worst in cultivation; or, with greater exactness, where there is competition for the tenancy the rent is equal to the whole of the produce less the working expenses. It is the surplus, great or small, which labour yields when aided by the greater or less fertility of the natural agents.

From what precedes we may draw two very important conclusions. The first of these is that a rise in the price of agricultural produce is not, as is generally believed, the consequence of the rise of rents, but has this as its result. It is only when the farmer sells his corn and cattle dearer that he can pay a higher rental. Secondly, we may say that in all societies where wealth and population are developing, rents also tend to increase. In France and Belgium the average rent of land has almost doubled in the last fifty years. In England, also, the same tendency has shown itself, although during the last ten years it has been held in abeyance.

A rise in prices favours the increase of rent in two ways; firstly, the cultivator need sell less of his produce to cover his expenses; secondly, each article of produce sells more dearly. The fall of prices naturally acts in the contrary way.

Increase of rent is stopped, in the first place, by

all agricultural improvements whose effect is to increase production, and, secondly, by the facilities for foreign importation. These two causes lead to the same result—a greater abundance of produce— and from this comes a fall of prices, and a consequent fall of rents. At the same time it is quite possible that an increased quantity of produc's, even when sold at a lower price, will yield an equal or greater total. In this case rents will not fall, and may even rise.

Agricultural improvements, such as better ploughs and reaping machines, new highways, &c., which diminish the cost of production without increasing the total amount of products brought into the market, have a uniform tendency to raise rents. It is to this, together with the increase in the prices of meat and butter, that recently the rise of rent has generally been due.

§ 3. Arguments of Economists who Deny the Existence of Rent.

Certain economists, disciples of Bastiat and Carey, deny the existence of rent. The share of nature in production, says Bastiat, is always given gratuitously. If a rental is paid it is as a return for the labour and capital which have been sunk in the earth, and not for its natural fertility. Carey adds, contrary to the theory of Ricardo, it is the light land of the hills that are first cultivated, and only afterwards the more fertile districts of the valley.

Bastiat's statement is opposed to facts. The lands which yield the highest rent in virtue of returning the largest amount of produce with the least expense are often those in which the least human labour has been sunk. Such are the rich pasture-lands of Normandy, the soil of Egypt, and the " black lands" of Russia and Roumania. You have only to ask a farmer to be told that one field in a farm can often pay twice the rent of another. The Clos-Vougeot, the Château-Lafitte, the Johannisberg, yield a rent ten times as high as that of neighbouring vineyards which have required the same amount of labour. The European rivers in which salmon is caught pay a very considerable rent. There are many sources of utilities which bear a price which owe their value entirely to nature.

The remark of Carey, on the other hand, has some foundation, but it does not weaken the principle of Ricardo's theory. Men have cultivated the most fertile or best situated lands first *among those within their reach.* For them other lands had no existence. When, later on, these other lands came into the market, they had the effect of an agricultural improvement. By yielding more abundant produce they momentarily arrested the rise of rents; but where they were of exceptional fertility they must themselves have paid a heavy rent from the first. Soon, wealth and population continuing to increase, the rents of all the lands increase also. On this point Ricardo is in the right.

CHAPTER V.

WAGES.

WAGES are the reward of labour.

Wages reckoned in money must not be confounded with wages calculated by the amount of commodities this money will procure. A workman can barely live in London on half-a-crown a day, because board and lodging are both very dear. In China or Japan with a third of this sum he need want for nothing, because everything is cheap.

What is important to the labourer is the amount of commodities, such as bread, meat, and clothing, which his wage will allow him to consume. A decrease in the cost of production, causing a fall in the price of products, tends indirectly to increase wages. The labourer does not receive more money, but for the same money gets more commodities.

§ 1. Systems of Remuneration.

Labourers are usually paid in money, but sometimes in kind, as in countries where the farm hands are still boarded by their master.

Labour may be paid according to time—by the day or hour; or according to the work done—by the job or piece, as when painters are paid by the square yard, or masons by the cubic foot. Payment

by the piece is preferable for many reasons.   In
the first place it is fairer ; every one is paid according
to his skill and his industry.   Again, it stimulates
activity by bringing home the feeling of responsibility
—the mainspring of the economic world.   Thus the
total production is increased, and the cost of supervision abolished.   If the workman is not tied down
to a machine piecework enables him to choose his
own hours, and to become, in a small way, a contractor himself, since all piecework is of the nature
of a contract.   On the other hand, it is of great
advantage to the master, who has only to pay for
what he actually receives.

In spite of these advantages workmen dislike the
introduction of piecework.   In England they have
often struck against it.   In France, after the
Revolution of 1848, they even demanded that it
should be forbidden by law.   They contend that
the price of piecework is reckoned by what a " crack "
workman can do, and that, consequently, an
ordinary workman cannot earn a living.   In reality
work by the piece is, as a rule, better paid than
work by the day, except when employers are compelled by competition either to reduce the rate or
stop work altogether.   It is to be wished that the
system of piecework should prevail as widely as
possible, inasmuch as by considerably increasing
production it must indirectly promote the prosperity
of the working classes.

A still greater stimulus to work and to the

improvement of the labourer's condition is afforded
by adding to wages a certain share in the profits. It
is now very usual to grant such a share to the
manager and head-workmen in a commercial company in order to interest them in its success, and
thus increase their zeal. The best results would
follow if this system could be extended to all the
workmen.

In France, Germany, Holland, and Switzerland,
by a happy idea, some employers, instead of immediately handing over to their workmen this
addition to their pay, save it so as to provide them
with a fund for their old age.

§ 2. The Iron Law.

" In all kinds of work," says Turgot, " it must, and
does, come to pass that a workman's wages are
limited to what is needful for his subsistence."
Later on Ricardo reproduced this idea, and believed
that he had demonstrated its truth beyond contradiction. The wages of a workman, he says,
naturally reduce themselves to what is indispensable
if he is to live and support a family. He cannot
be content with less, for excess of destitution
diminishes the number of workmen, and the fewer
the hands the higher the wages. Neither can he
for any length of time obtain more; for easier
circumstances increases the number of marriages
and births, so that there are soon more hands in the

market, and wages return to the necessary or natural minimum.

Lassalle, a leader among the German socialists, appealing to Ricardo and the majority of economists, exclaims, " Here is the iron law, formulated by the masters of political economy, a law which condemns workmen to irremediable misery. A society which culminates in such an iniquity must be profoundly modified ! "

Happily the observation of facts does not confirm the truth of Ricardo's supposed law. It has been abundantly proved that throughout Europe the condition of the working classes has considerably improved during the last century. Far from producing an excessive increase of population, easier circumstances tend to moderate it by the effect of prudence. Misery, on the other hand, has ever been prolific, as has been proved in Ireland, and as is indicated by the ill-omened word " proletariate," which means at once the miserable class, and the class that is overburdened with children.

Labour, prosperity, and virtue, working together under the reign of justice, will effectually abolish the iron law.

§ 3. Causes of Different Rates of Wages.

Wages are very different in the various occupations. A diamond-cutter in Amsterdam earns a pound a day ; an agricultural labourer in the same country little over a shilling.

Many causes give rise to exceptional wages.

(1) *Rare Ability of Certain Kinds.*—This constitutes a sort of monopoly. A great singer earns more than £5,000 a year, which is too much. Again, in a different rank, glass blowers who make the large panes of glass earn their ten shillings a day.

(2) *Locality.*—Nominal wages are dearer in town because living is dearer.

(3) *The Average Length of the Working Season.*— A workman who can only ply his trade during a part of the year must earn higher wages when he does work or he could not make both ends meet. Masons, in countries where the work is interrupted by frosts, are an example of this.

(4) *The Repugnant Element in Certain Occupations.*—No one would submit to this except for unusually high pay. The hangman is well paid, though he works but rarely. In many occupations, on the other hand, the certainty or agreeable character of the work compensate for the smallness of the remuneration. A junior clerk is contented with a slender salary because his future is assured. Governesses, if one may judge by advertisements, often ask only for "a comfortable home," and no salary.

(5) *The Length of the Apprenticeship.*—This insures a high salary in certain occupations, for part of the salary goes towards repaying the expenses which have been incurred.

The old economists thought that, taking these

L

differences into consideration, wages might be said to tend towards a uniform rate. Certainly, other things being equal, an exceptionally high salary must attract workers in such numbers as to cause a reduction; whereas an exceptionally low salary will make the workmen seek trades where the pay is better. Nevertheless, as Mr. Cliffe Leslie has shown by numerous examples, wages in the same country and for the same trade will vary considerably according to the locality. Love of home, habit, the difficulty of moving and finding houseroom, and sometimes differences of dialect, are all obstacles to a uniform rate of wages. In France, in the neighbourhood of Paris, a journeyman can earn twice as much as in the midlands, and in Belgium, out of two country districts, in one, the Campine, he gains a shilling a day, in the other, the Ardennes, nearly half-a-crown!

§ 4. Low Wages not a Cause of Cheap Work.

The great railway contractor, Mr. Brassey, after having employed labourers in every country in the world, has written a book, called *Work and Wages*, to prove that cheapness of work is obtained by paying good wages. An ill-paid workman is weak and indolent; the work hangs fire and ends by costing dear. Mr. Brassey's advice is to insist on energy and industry, and pay well. Every one will benefit by this system, workman, employer, and society at large.

§ 5. The Wages Fund.

Many economists have believed that in every country, at any given moment, there exists a fund specially devoted to the reward of labour. In this way an average rate of wages is imposed upon all alike, and this of necessity, since when each workman takes his share of the fund, the value of the share is the result of the amount of the fund divided by the number of the workmen. Neither the resistance of the workmen nor the watchfulness of the master can modify this mathematical law. If you give more to one, there will be less for the others. The average rate of wages will only increase, if the wages fund increase more rapidly than the number of the workmen.

The truth of the matter is as follows. The nation lives on the sum total of the useful articles which it produces. It cannot consume more than this, but the manner in which this fund is divided between rent, interest, wages and profits, depends on contracts, custom, and the will of the parties concerned. The one thing true is that if one of these parties obtains more, one or all of the others will have less.

In this way since 1870, the extraordinary activity of industries in Europe has occasioned a general rise of wages. It is rent which since this date has been diminished.

The problem may be presented in the following form :

Product = Rent + Interest + Wages + Profits.

If the share assigned to wages is increased, the balance which is divided among the other participators must diminish, for Product — Wages = Rent + Interest + Profits. To take a more simple proof: a market gardener who pays two shillings a day to the labourer he employs on a garden which brings in four shillings a day will have two shillings to keep for himself. If he is obliged to pay his labourer three shillings, plainly he himself will only have one.

§ 6. Is there a Natural or Normal Wage?

Economists of the school of Ricardo maintain that there is a natural rate of wages, which is determined, like the price of any other commodity, by the cost of production of labour.

The cost of production of the commodity labour is the sum which is absolutely necessary to enable the labourer to live and work.

Undoubtedly wages have often been as low as this, and history teaches us that frequently they have not even sufficed to support the labourer, since whole populations were decimated by famine, as in the reigns of Louis XIV. and Louis XV. But this was the effect of detestable institutions and of human ignorance, not of any so-called natural laws.

The normal rate of wages is that which, at the least, supplies the labourer and his family with the means of subsistence, and of the normal development of the faculties of body and mind.

If it be asked " Who shall determine the sum

which this subsistence and the normal development of the faculties demand ?" I answer "The science of health." This problem, so often declared insoluble, is solved every day in the administration of the army in the different countries. This administration fixes the amount of nourishment and the quality of the clothes necessary to keep the soldier's powers in good condition. Ought not the labourer to be able to earn by his work at least the rations of a soldier?

§ 7. The Causes which fix the Rate of Wages.

Are wages, as some economists assert, in proportion to the productiveness of labour? It would seem that they ought to be so. If labour produced twice the amount of useful articles, surely the labourer ought to be twice as well off. This, however, is not the case, except when he is also the possessor of the capital, as in the instance of the peasant proprietor.

The pay given simply as wages is determined by other causes. The increase of production profits, in the first place, the manufacturer, and subsequently, by the fall of prices, the general public. A manufacturer sets up in his factory a machine which enables the workman to produce each day ten times as much as he could do by hand; if no greater dexterity is required from him his wages will not be increased. All the advantage of the machine will go to the manufacturer, until there comes a fall of prices consequent upon the increased ease and abundance of production. Again, by giving his orchard a double layer of manure a market gardener may double his crop of apples. He will not make this a reason for paying high wages to the labourers who gather them, though their *real* wages may incidentally be increased by the fall in the price of apples.

It is plain that the productiveness of labour only acts indirectly on its market value by multiplying useful objects, and thus enabling the wage earners to buy more of them.

What regulates wages is the competition between the labourers offering their work and the masters in need of it. As Cobden said with great force, when two workmen are running after one master, wages fall; when two masters are running after one workman, wages rise. In other words, wages are subject to the great law of supply and demand which will be explained later on.

To this rise and fall of wages, however, there are certain limits. They cannot fall below what is absolutely necessary for the labourer to subsist; in that case he would disappear altogether. On the other hand, they cannot rise beyond the total of the value added to the object. As has been well observed, the piece of work which is only just worth doing brings in very little, and if the wages to be paid exceed this little, the work will never be ordered or bought.

A journeyman shoemaker makes a pair of shoes worth eight shillings with leather worth three; under no circumstances can his pay exceed five shillings. From the increase of value created by the wage-earner, something must be deducted to reward the employer and the capitalist, or the one would cease to employ workmen, and the other to advance money.

With the reward of his labour, say Proudhon and Karl Marx, the workman cannot buy back the product of his labour; he is therefore robbed by the capitalist. The socialists who talk thus make an error of calculation. The object has not been produced solely by the exertion of the workman, but by his exertions aided by tools and employed on raw materials. It is true that labour alone is active, but it only becomes productive by the cooperation of capital and nature. This cooperation has an equal right to reward. If the workman can make himself the proprietor of the tools and materials he requires in his work, he will be able to keep the whole of the product. The aim of the wage-earner must therefore be to become a proprietor.

Wages rise when a large number of workmen are required, and this is the case when industrious and enterprising persons abound, and there is plenty of capital. The way, therefore, to improve the condition of the working classes is to encourage the creation of capital by thrift and the development of education and the spirit of enterprise. On the other hand, wages diminish when the numbers of the workmen are increasing more rapidly than the undertakings and capital which can employ them. Here we touch on what is called the population question.

The competition between masters requiring workmen, on the one side, and workmen requiring
masters, on the other, only influences each branch of
labour separately. A demand for a number of tailors
will raise the wages of tailors but not those of other
trades. Nevertheless if several industries are simultaneously so prosperous as to require a large number
of workmen, for a time the rise of wages will spread
by degrees up to a certain point, inasmuch as the
rush of workmen to these trades will cause a
deficiency in others.

§ 8. Has the Condition of the Working Classes Improved ?

No one will maintain that the condition of those
who work with their hands is all that it should be,
but it is certain that it has improved and is still
improving every day. Let any one who has doubts
on this subject enter the cottage of the worst paid
agricultural labourer, and examine his food and
clothing, utensils and furniture, and then let him
read the famous passage in which La Bruyère
described the French peasantry of the reign of
Louis XIV.

"Spread over the country are to be seen certain
wild animals, of either sex, black, livid and sun-
scorched, chained to the earth which they dig and
turn with unyielding persistency. They have what
may be called an articulate voice ; when standing
erect they show a human face ; in fact they are men.

At night they retire to their dens, where they live on black bread, water, and roots. They spare other men the trouble of sowing, digging and reaping for their food, and so ought not to lack this bread which they have sown."

In 1740 Massillon, Bishop of Clermont-Ferrand, wrote to Cardinal Fleury, Prime Minister of Louis XV: "The country people live in frightful misery, without beds, without furniture; one half of the year, the greater part of them eat hay and barley-bread, their only food, and this they are obliged to snatch from their children's mouths, to pay the taxes."

When we think of the time when men died of hunger in crowds along the high roads, we shall see no reason to despair of our own days, while we hope still better things for the next century.

CHAPTER VI.

MEANS OF IMPROVING THE CONDITION OF WAGE EARNERS.

In past centuries the rich and powerful always sought to reduce the share of the labourers in order to increase their own. Our own century, however, appears to have undertaken the duty pointed out by the famous reformer, Saint-Simon, of improving the material, intellectual, and moral condition of the working class.   The means of arriving at this result is nothing less than the social problem of the day. Let us examine some of the solutions proposed.

§ 1. Charity.

Formerly benevolence knew but one way of assisting those who were called "the poor," namely, by almsgiving, and in their sublime enthusiasm the charitable would sometimes go the length of abandoning all they had to embrace voluntary poverty. But economic analysis has demonstrated that almsgiving mulcts labour for the support of needy idleness. It diminishes responsibility and self-respect, weakens the incentive to activity, and thus only fosters misery. Of this the effect of the daily distributions of food made by the convents under the old system furnishes an ample proof.

There will always be involuntary misfortunates to relieve, but it is not to charity that we must look for the final improvement of the lot of the majority.

§ 2. Communism.

Communism has alternately been the war-cry of the oppressed, as in the insurrections of Spartacus, Wat Tyler, the Jacquerie, and the peasants in the time of Luther, or the dream of some great mind, as with Plato in the *Republic*, Sir Thomas More in the *Utopia* (1516), Campenella in the *Civitas Solis* (1620), and Fénelon in the *Salente* of the *Télémaque*.

The Essenes in Judæa, the disciples of Pythagoras

in Magna Graecia, the first Christians in Jerusalem,
were alike in having all things in common, and in
our own day monastic societies multiply on the Continent with their vows to annul the distinction
between " mine " and "thine." We have here the
application of the saying of J. J. Rousseau, " Beware
of forgetting that the fruits of the earth are every
one's, and the earth itself no one's."

In this system the means of production are the
property of the society. The principle which governs
the division of the produce is the rule, " From each
according to his strength, and to each according to
his needs." The society constituted on this basis
would be the copy of the family economy, in which
each member does actually labour as much as he can,
and consume as much as he wants.

Communism, however, will never attain permanence, since it violates justice and despises the
deepest instincts of man's nature. The formula of
justice is *Cuique suum,* " to every man his own," or
" to each according to his works." Communism, on
the contrary, takes no account of works, and recog-
nises no " his own." The industrious are made the
dupes of the sluggards who trade upon them.

The spring of human activity is always and everywhere self-interest. In communism self-interest is
continually sacrificed; if it acts at all it is to impel
men to sloth and gluttony, for where needs are the
measure of rights, that man will look out best for
himself who shall eat the most and work the least.

If convents continue and even increase, it is only by uprooting from the hearts of their inmates the deepest of natural feelings, the craving for independence, the love of self, and family affections. It is the hope of heavenly happiness that works the miracle. Egoism is not really dead, for it endures as long as life; but its aim has been transferred to another world. Who can believe that an industrial society can be organised on the principles and the plan of a convent? "Communism," said the socialist Proudhon, "means the disregard of work, the weariness of life, suppression of thought, destruction of the self, and affirmation of chaos."

§ 3. Nihilism.

A Russian revolutionist, Bakounine, comes before us with the assertion : the labourer is robbed, crushed, reduced to misery by all those institutions which take the assurance of his welfare as their mission, the state, royalty, religion, the army, property, and the family. Man will only be free and happy when of existing society not one stone shall rest upon another. Everything must be annihilated: *nihil*, "nothing," this is the goal. Nihilism will bring salvation.

If he be asked what new organisation it is proposed to adopt, Bakounine replies that he interdicts both himself and us from seeking one. Every utopist is a tyrant, for he would like to impose the organisation which he believes the best. The gospel of nihilism is " shapelessness," that is to say, the absence of any social organisation; the one best adapted to enfranchised humanity will spring spontaneously from the people.

The ascetics of the first centuries of Christianity, and the believers in the millennium, thinking society irretrievably abandoned to wickedness, expected its renovation from a cosmic cataclysm. Out of the fire that consumed the world were to issue " a new heaven and a new earth." Justice would triumph, and the reign of Right begin. Rousseau, in his despair of remedying our vices and iniquities, would lead humanity back to its primitive forest. It is the same sentiment, pushed to the verge of madness, which gives birth to nihilism. Such a doctrine there is no need to combat. Indeed, how is it possible to argue against and refute "that which is not " ?

§ 4. Anarchy.

Among existing socialists many call themselves anarchists, that is to say, adversaries of every form of government, from the Greek word, ἀναρχία, which means " the absence of a governing power."

If these socialists simply aim at reducing the powers of the state to a minimum, they are, in this, in agreement with the " non-interference " school of economists. If they really take the suppression of the state as their aim, they must wish to lead us back to a condition of prehistoric savagery, in which, in the absence of all law and authority, violence

carries the day, and the weak, as among animals, are
devoured by the strong.

§ 5. Collectivism and the Organisation of Labour.

Existing socialists reject communism, but preach
the gospel of collectivism. Like communism, collectivism assigns to society the possession of the
materials of production, and the instruments of
labour, that is to say, land, mines, railways, and tools
of all sorts. In the division, however, of the produce,
they admit the principle of a reward proportionate
to the work done, and in this way do not suppress
responsibility or the stimulus of private interest.
But who is to be the proprietor of the means of
production, the state, the commune, or the corporation of workmen ? The system is so imperfectly
formulated that it is difficult to discuss.

In his famous book, *L'Organisation du Travail*, M.
Louis Blanc proposed that all industries should be
functions of the state, as is the case at present with
the working of the railways in Belgium, and this is,
roughly speaking, the proposal of the collectivists of
to-day. If it were adopted it would follow that
every one would be a Civil servant, and that the
whole society would be organised like an army.
At present the workman who does not work is
dismissed. If all industries were in the hand of the
state, dismissal would be no longer possible. It
would have to be replaced by the police-cell or the

prison. The spring of productive activity would no longer be the initiative of the individual, but passive obedience and compulsion.

Industrial progress is attained under the present system, because every manufacturer endeavours to make cheaply and sell largely, so as to make larger profits. But who would find it his interest to improve its processes of production, if every one were paid by a salary?

The cessation of progress and a universal despotism regulating every action of the economic life, that is what would be the world's condition!

§ 6. Cooperative Societies.

In a cooperative society for production the workmen supply at once the capital and labour, and the union of these two factors in the same hands brings the antagonism between capitalist and labourer to a natural end. It has been thought to find in this union the solution of the social conflict. Unfortunately the management of an industrial undertaking is a difficult task. The majority of workmen are as yet incapable of it, and any adequate remuneration to the managers and head *employés* appears to them a violation of the principle of equality. Cooperative societies have generally failed owing to the incapacity or dishonesty of the managers. A joint-stock company with the workmen as shareholders, would offer the same advantages, and probably succeed better.

It must not be forgotten that in the economic

world, just as in the political, authority is indispensable. In a manufactory, as on board ship or in the state, there must be a master in command, and subordinates to obey him ; if not, we have a condition of anarchy, disorder and ruin. Up to the present workmen who choose their masters show themselves as ignorant of how to obey them as soldiers who elect their captain.

§ 7. Emigration.

Emigration only brings about a rise of wages when it abruptly carries off a large part of the population without disturbing industry, as in the " exodus " which, after the famine of 1847, carried off from Ireland three of its eight millions of inhabitants. Slow emigration, like that which ships from Germany its one to two hundred thousands a year, has no effect on wages beyond preventing their decrease. The births fill up the void ; and in the absence of any diminution in the supply of hands, wages do not increase.

§ 8. Corporations and Trades Unions.

Formerly the workmen of any given trade formed a close corporation, admission to which could only be obtained after a long apprenticeship and severe tests. In this way no one not a member of the corporation of locksmiths might make a lock. The performance of certain kinds of work was a monopoly. A man was permitted to starve, but not to earn a livelihood by his skill. In the edict of 1776 Turgot affirmed, "The right to labour is the possession of all, and the first and most inalienable of all possessions."

Nowadays the old corporations have disappeared, but the enfranchised workmen finding themselves weak in their individual isolation, have once more banded themselves together according to their crafts, though in no case with any exclusive privileges. These "Trade Unions" reckon a considerable number of members in England and America. By means of a weekly payment they form a relief-fund, and assemble for deliberation and common action towards raising wages. Their weapons are coalitions and strikes.

§ 9. Coalitions and Strikes.

Workmen from time to time endeavour to obtain an increase of wages by coalescing to exact it and refusing to labour, that is to say by going out on strike if their demands are not satisfied. Strikes are of common occurrence in England—2,352 in the ten years 1870-1879—inasmuch as the workmen associated in the trades unions, by means of weekly contributions form a fund which is employed, at need, for the support of the men on strike.

The strike is organised in one manufactory, in the others the workmen continue to labour and pay wages to those out of employ. In the end the employer is compelled to yield. In order to avoid being thus one by one beset and reduced to terms,

M

the masters reply to the strike by the lock-out, that is to say by a complete stoppage of work, a step which forces the workmen to speedy submission, for want of funds to maintain the struggle.

These strikes are the cause of great suffering, especially to the workmen. Mr. Bevan, a statistician, has calculated that one hundred and twelve strikes have cost as many millions by loss of wages. Sometimes, in certain localities, they have destroyed an industry altogether.

Strikes can only raise wages when economic laws permit, that is to say, when profits are high ; on the Continent they more often only take place when the manufacturers are reduced to extremity and cannot pay labour better without ruining themselves, and, as a result, rendering the lot of their workmen still worse.

To avoid strikes recourse is now had in England to two expedients.

(1) Arbitration, in which masters and workmen lay their arguments before a competent judge, who is chosen by agreement to decide the dispute.

(2) The fixing of wages according to the selling price of the produce, by what is called the sliding scale. Example : a rise or fall in the price of iron effects a proportionate rise or fall in the wages of the workmen who produce it.

§ 10. Increase of Capital and Diffusion of Property.

Economists assert that the only means to improve the condition of the labourer is to increase capital. The increase of capital, if not accompanied by an increase in the number of workmen, will have as its effect a rise of wages. Nothing can be more exact than this statement; but the means it describes are insufficient. The growth of capital has a limit, and this limit is conceivably attainable. We can already catch a glimpse of it, though the reward of labour has none the less failed to become sufficient. What is needed is that the increment of capital should pass in a great part, into the hands of the labourers themselves by the help of good laws and thrift.

Thus to preach thrift to those who, it is owned, have not even enough for necessities, may seem at first a cruel mockery. It is true that they lack necessaries; yet how much money they spend on such, to them, deadly superfluities as alcohol and tobacco! If workmen would save only the vast sums which they devote to the alcoholic beverages which brutalise them, in twenty years they could buy every factory at which they work. It is thus from the practice of certain virtues such as prudence, continence, and sobriety, that help can alone arrive.

§ 11. The Relation Between the Rise of Wages and the Increase of Population.

If population increase more rapidly than capital, and above all, than the means of subsistence, no reform can permanently improve the lot of the poorest classes, for the fairest division of the produce will only yield to each of them an insufficient reward.

J. S. Mill is therefore right in his assertion that in political economy the question of population dominates every other.

CHAPTER VII.

ON THE INCREASE OF POPULATION.

Is the increase of population to be dreaded? Two opposite opinions have long existed on this subject. In the cities of ancient Greece, where space was limited, philosophers, politicians, and legislators, believed that the increase of the number of citizens was an evil which had to be remedied, even by means which make us shudder. In Rome, on the other hand, where the want of men was felt, large families were honoured and celibates punished. So too in the seventeenth and eighteenth centuries when the country was nearly everywhere depopulated by despotic governments, it was thought

necessary to favour in every way the multiplication
of the human race. Thus we find Montesquieu
saying that, " population is always a gain," and
Rousseau that, " there is no worse dearth for a
nation than that of men."

Most economists, however, agree with the opinion
that " it is more necessary to multiply the means of
subsistence than men," and are concerned at too
prolific marriages, because they increase the number
of mouths to fill, while politicians and conquest-
loving kings rejoice at them, as swelling the
numbers of their soldiers.

Malthus, whose name is inseparably connected
with this question, has expounded in two thick
volumes the following theory. The human race
tends to increase more rapidly than the means of
subsistence. It advances in a geometrical progression
by continuous multiplication, like the numbers—

$$2 \times 2 = 4 \times 2 = 8 \times 2 = 16 \times 2 = 32 \times 2 = 64.$$

The means of subsistence, on the contrary, increase
in an arithmetical progression by continuous addition,
like the numbers—

$$2 + 2 = 4 + 2 = 6 + 2 = 8 + 2 = 10 + 2 = 12,$$

and thus equilibrium soon ceases to exist between
the number of mouths to fill and the amount of
nourishment available to fill them. If these two
laws of progression are not in reality observed, it
is because the increase of population is stopped by
certain repressive forces. But these forces are the

very scourges under which humanity groans, such as disease, famine, war, and, above all, misery. To escape these the only way is to arrest the excessive multiplication of the race by moral constraint.

While abandoning the mathematical formulas of Malthus, J. S. Mill has re-stated his theory in the following propositions, which appear unassailable. The human race, when not odiously ill-governed, tends to increase. As a matter of fact, it doubles its numbers within a period which varies in each country. This period is of about 30 years for the United States and Java, and from 125 to 150 for France; the annual increase per 10,000 inhabitants being 26 for France, 98 for Belgium, 101 for England, 115 for Germany, and 260 for the United States. On the other hand, the number of acres of arable land is limited in each country, and in the earth as a whole, and the quantity of food which each acre is capable of producing can only increase in a certain measure. Thus a want of equilibrium must sooner or later occur between the increase of the race, which is unlimited, and the increase of food, which is limited. The time when this want of equilibrium will produce a famine is doubtless distant; but long before this last extremity is reached, the increasing demand for the agricultural produce won from the limited soil will cause a rise of prices and a greater difficulty in living which will only be diminished, even momentarily, by improvements in the art of agriculture.

Many writers have rejected these gloomy forebodings. Here are some of their objections.

(1) Matter, says Carey, takes the form of lower organisms more easily than that of higher. Therefore there will always be more herbs and roots than bullocks and sheep, and more bullocks and sheep than men. A manifest error, for already in densely populated countries, there is not enough meat produced for every one to have the quantity necessary for health.

(2) The density of population increases the productiveness of labour, by finding employment for more capital. This is true, but the question is not one of industrial products in general, but solely of food; and a hundred bales of cloth will not feed a single child.

(3) It is said that if we restore to the soil as much as is taken from it, a *circulus* is created, *i.e.* a circle of life from which humanity can always draw the means of maintaining its own. Here the advice is excellent. Let us restore to the earth even more than it gives us, and enrich it with elements of fertility extracted from inorganic substances. Nevertheless with too much manure the corn lies and rots; and here we find our limit.

(4) The world has innumerable fertile plains unoccupied, to which the inhabitants of countries where the population is too dense can emigrate. It has been calculated that there is abundant space on our planet for twelve thousand million human beings,

and there are not as many as fifteen hundred millions
in existence.   Moreover commerce, in its ever-de-
veloping freedom and activity, brings to the countries
of our old continent the products of all the virgin
soils in increasing quantities.   All this is true, but it
does not upset the other truth, demonstrated by J. S.
Mill, that if population always continues to increase,
the time must come when the most perfect system of
agriculture will be unable to produce sufficient food.
Such a state of things has been already reached in
Flanders, with its more than two inhabitants to every
acre, and in Oudh in India, where the population is
almost equally dense.

Is there then no loop-hole?   Will men grow too
numerous and be reduced to devour each other for
lack of food, and shall our race at the end of this
progressive development of which it is so proud, end,
as it began, in simple cannibalism?   Not so; but it
will find a refuge in that true progress which may be
summed up in the three words, more light, more
virtue, more justice.

Increase of light will make the life of the spirit
triumph over that of the brute that is in us.   Increase of virtue will lead us to greater prudence and
continence.   Lastly, increase of justice, by securing
to each man the full enjoyment of the fruits of his
labour, will make proprietorship more general, and
so supply the well-attested antidote to the excessive
multiplication of our species.

CHAPTER VIII.

PROFIT.

§ 1. Meaning and Reason of Profit.

PROFIT is the reward of the labour of the employer. This reward is uncertain, variable, speculative ; for the employer disburses fixed sums for rent, wages, and interest, without knowing how much the sale of his productions will return him. At the end of the year he calculates the total cost of his business, and deducts this from the sum of his receipts. The difference is his profit. Profit is, therefore, the surplus of the price obtained for productions over the costs of all kinds which have been incurred in creating them.

There are two elements in profit. The first rewards the skill and energy of the proprietor, and therefore increases in proportion to the greater knowledge and preparation which an industry demands, and the fewer attractions it possesses. It varies greatly in every industry according to the qualities of the individual proprietors, for it is on these that success principally depends, so that where one man is ruined, another makes a fortune.

The second element is risk. The farmer sows a field without any means of knowing what the crop will be worth, or whether it will not be destroyed by hail. The incidental risks must be covered by a premium of insurance which goes to increase the profit; the more risky the undertaking the greater ought the profit to be.

Profits will tend to a uniform level in all the different industries, inasmuch as enterprising men of business, furnished with fresh supplies of capital, engage in such industries as offer any unusual returns. This levelling process, however, is never accurately effected, since the fluctuations of industry and trade cause perpetual variations in the rate of profits.

§ 2. Is the rate of Interest in Inverse Proportion to the rate of Wages?

Considering the wealth produced as a fixed quantity, Ricardo and his school have deduced from this that profits can only increase at the expense of wages. If an employer can pay exceptionally low wages, it is certain that the decrease in his expenses will increase his profit. His competitors, however, will soon obtain the some advantage, and the diminution in the cost of production will be followed by a fall of the selling price, and profits return to their former rate.

The truth of the matter is rather that profit, being also the reward of labour, will rise and fall simultaneously with wages. Where large profits are made the workmen can and ought to be well paid. In the United States profit and wages are high. In the States of Western Europe they are both much lower.

§ 3. Profits tend to Diminish.

The greater the productiveness of labour, the better will both master and workmen be rewarded by the large products which it creates. In a new country where the sources of wealth are numerous and little worked, masters and workmen can make large gains. In an old country, where every source has already been worked, persistent labour is needed for a livelihood, and skill or exceptional good fortune to make a fortune. Profits thus tend to diminish in proportion as the field of employment is limited when compared with the number of those who seek to employ their faculties, their arms, and capital.

The fall of profits is arrested by every improvement in the processes of labour by which it is enabled to produce more at a less cost. Railroads, for example, have given many people the opportunity of enriching themselves. In this may be seen the benefits which science confers alike upon master and man.

CHAPTER IX.

THE REWARD OF CAPITAL.

§ 1. What Interest is.

THE third factor which contributes to production is capital, and this, like the others, must be rewarded. The reward which it receives is called interest.

For replaceable and circulating capital, which is consumed by the borrower, interest is usually reckoned at so much per cent. the year, *e.g.* five pounds for a year's loan of a hundred. For fixed capital which the borrower has to return in its original form, the reward is proportionate to the service rendered and the probable depreciation.

Two elements may be distinguished in the interest which is paid for the enjoyment of a capital : the first, an insurance premium to cover the risk of loss; the second, simply the hire of the capital. In a country where there are bad laws and bad judges, the lender of capital runs the risk of never recovering it ; he will therefore stipulate for a premium at a sufficiently high percentage to at least cover this risk. It is for this reason that the rate of interest is always very high in the East—as much as fifteen or twenty per cent., or even more. The only means of reducing it is to make good laws and appoint upright judges.

The lender deprives himself of the use of his capital ; the borrower enjoys and profits by it. It is therefore only natural that the second should pay the first an idemnity, or hire, for this enjoyment. This is the second element of interest.

The rate of this hire will be high if there are few lenders compared to the number of borrowers, low if there are many lenders and few borrowers; and this in accordance with the general law of supply and demand. Lenders in search of an investment will be numerous when there are many persons rich enough to be able to save, and sufficiently economical to wish to do so. In Holland in the seventeenth century interest had fallen to three and even two per cent. Every one worked and traded, and no one spent all his income. Descartes was greatly struck at this circumstance. *Ibi nemo qui non excrcet mercaturam,* was his exclamation. Borrowers, on the other hand, abound when the spirit of enterprise is developed, and at the same time nature offers numerous remunerative employments to industry. In the United States, the majority of undertakings, such as the cultivation of virgin soils, the purchase of building ground, construction of houses, mines, factories and railways, yield profits as large as ten, twenty, or thirty per cent. Although, therefore, there is no deficiency of capital, enterprising men are ready to pay six and eight per cent. a year for the use of it. Great fortunes are quickly made, and several cases might be cited of twenty millions sterling having been accumulated in a few years.

§ 2. Interest tends to Diminish.

In countries like England where there is a dense population and wealth has long been abundant, the rate of interest tends to diminish for two reasons; in the first place, because the value of capitals which thrift is continually creating is reduced by their competition, and, in the second, because the fields of employment, *i.e.* the improvable sources of wealth, are ever diminishing.

The means of arresting this tendency of the rate
of interest in rich countries to fall, would be the
employment of capital in foreign investments, the
discovery of new sources of wealth, or the progress
of industry in certain directions, which, as in the case
of railroads, require costly but remunerative advances.
From 1850 to 1870 the rate of interest rose in
Europe because all over the world electric telegraphs,
both inland and submarine, railroads, canals for
transport and irrigation, new factories, banks, gas
companies, and profitable enterprises of all sorts
were able to use and richly reward all the capital that
was amassed.

When everywhere all the great undertakings shall
have been accomplished, and every industry have the
most perfect means of production at its disposal, the
time will come when new capital will no longer find
remunerative employment. This is what J. S. Mill
calls the stationary state, and he regards it as a
happy one for humanity, which, he says, has not been
created to weary itself for ever in the pursuit of
wealth ; and Mill is right. The life truly worthy of
our high destinies is that of the Athenian citizen in
the time of Socrates, occupied in philosophy, art and
public affairs, but with the added condition that the
one half of the day shall be devoted to some sort of
productive labour.

The extreme limit to the fall of interest is the
point at which the reward of thrift shall become
insufficient to cause the renunciation of the immediate

consumption of the wealth produced. When a saving of a hundred pounds shall bring in no more than **ten shillings** the year, the number of savers will greatly diminish, though we should not forget that simple anxiety for the future is often a sufficient inducement to cause money to be hoarded in a chest, where it will bear no interest at all.

When the reward of capital shall no longer be sufficient to attract to new savings, the time will also have come when humanity will have at its disposal all the necessary means of production, and so long as it keeps these in good repair it will be able to devote the whole product of each year's labour to immediate enjoyment. This time is still far distant.

§ 3. The Lawfulness of Interest, and the Laws against Usury.

Moral sentiment throughout antiquity, Aristotle, the fathers of the Church, and ecclesiastical law, have united in condemning all interest in the severest terms as a theft and even a homicide. Cato remarked : *Majores ita in legibus posuerunt furem dupli condemnari, fenatorem quadrupli*—"The laws of our fathers condemned the thief to restore double, and the usurer quadruple ;" and in his time it was still asked at Rome, *Quid est fenerari ? Quid est hominem occidere ?*—" What is lending at interest ? What killing a man ?"

This condemnation was dictated, in the first place,

by an error as to the nature of capital, in the second by the sight of the evils which actually resulted from lending at interest.

As regards the error as to the nature of capital, it was believed that capital consisted exclusively of silver and gold, which are "barren." "Interest," says Aristotle, "is money born of money, and of all acquisitions is the most unnatural." The same idea is found again at Rome: *Nummus non parit nummum—* "One coin does not give birth to another," and, truly enough, a sovereign will not at the end of a year produce a shilling to pay its hire.

The ancients, however, were deceived by appearances. Silver and gold, it is true, produce nothing, but they are only the means of reaching provisions, tools, machines—in a word, capital, which last is essentially productive, since it is, thanks to this, that anything is produced by labour. In the words used by Bentham in answer to Aristotle, "one gold daric cannot give birth to another, but with this piece of money I can buy a ram and a sheep which will yield me lambs, whence a whole flock may be born.

In ancient times the evils caused by the lending money at interest rendered the custom odious, because most often it was the wretched who borrowed for the means of subsistence, not to make a profit from the loan. The interest of the debt devoured the capital, and the borrower was soon reduced to misery and the mercy of his creditor. Such was the history of the plebeians at Rome. Whoever reads the Law of the

Twelve Tables will understand why, to escape their creditors, the people fled the city and took refuge on the sacred mount. Here is an extract on the subject :

Aeris confessi rebusque jure judicatis triginta dies justi sunt.	For the payment of an acknowledged debt, or a legal judgment, thirty days shall be allowed by law.
Post deinde manus injectio esto, in jus ducito.	On the expiry of these, the debtor shall be seized and brought before the magistrate.
Ni judicatum facit aut is endo em jure vindicit, vincito aut nervo aut compedibus quindecim pondo, ne minore, aut si volet majore vincito.	If he neither pay nor give surety for the amount, the creditor shall take him to his home, binding him either with thongs or with fetters of not less than fifteen pounds weight, and of more if he please.
Tertiis nundinis partes secanto, si plus minusve secuerint, se fraude esto.	After the third market day the creditors shall divide his body into portions, and if they cut more or less than their share they shall be free from blame.

Again, among the Israelites the lending money at interest was considered a means of ruin and persecution, and as such was forbidden between Jews, though allowed with respect to the stranger. Thus the canon law and the Fathers of the Church in condemning interest of every kind were only conforming to the idea of justice which prevailed on this subject in Greece, in Rome, and in the Old Testament.

Analysis proves that interest is at once just and necessary. It is just, because whoever creates a piece of capital, a plough, for example, has a right to be rewarded for the sacrifice which he makes in not consuming at his ease the provisions which have nourished him while he was making this new instrument of labour. If he lends his plough the borrower will obtain a greater profit than if he used a spade. Would it be fair that the borrower should retain the whole of this increased profit due to the employment of the more perfect instrument? The lender and borrower in such a transaction are two partners, and it is only just that they should share the advantage obtained. Interest is thus only the equivalent of the utility daily produced by the article of which the enjoyment is lent.

But interest is not only just, it is also necessary. Were it prohibited or suppressed no one would economise except to hoard; all savings, as in former times, would be deposited in strong boxes, and this reasonably, for why risk losing them without the chance of profit? Little new capital created, and no capital lent, would be the result produced.

Formerly in every country laws against usury forbade the exaction of what was considered excessive interest, that is to say, interest at more than five or six per cent. These laws have now been almost everywhere abolished, and rightly, for they were useless and even injurious to those whom they were meant to protect. Useless, because the lender eluded them by stipulating for a commission on each of the frequent renewals of the loan; injurious, because they increased the risk of lending with the inevitable result of raising the rate of interest.

§ 4. The Influence of the Abundance or Scarcity of Money on the Rate of Interest.

The manufacturer does not care about being able to hire the use of money, but of provisions, raw materials, tools, machinery, and everything which, when set at work by labour, produces useful objects. It is, nevertheless, by money or by notes on the security of money that possession of these instruments of production is attained; and it is under the form of money that loans are negotiated. Money is a circulating agent which makes things pass from one hand to another. It follows, that, if money is scarce the means of obtaining the capital necessary to production are more difficult of attainment and must be paid more dearly. Just as when ships are wanting to convey merchandise, freight charges are heavier, so, when the pecuniary means of transport are lacking, interest rises.

In so far as the possession of objects is passed from hand to hand by the employment of bills of exchange, the influence of the scarcity of coined money on the rate of interest is diminished. Again, if this scarcity continue, prices fall, and in this way each pecuniary means of transport transfers the possession of more articles, until the existing quantity of coined money is made sufficient, and its scarceness —the cause of the rise of interest—is no longer felt.

PART II.

THE CIRCULATION OF WEALTH.

WHEN each of the factors who have contributed to the creation of wealth, the landlord, the labourer, and the capitalist, has obtained his share, he uses it to procure the articles which he wishes to consume. In order that he may receive, he gives; wealth passes from hand to hand, and circulates by exchange.

CHAPTER I.

EXCHANGE.

§ 1. Barter.

THE simplest form of exchange is the barter of wares for wares. In prehistoric times only barter can have been in use, and this is still the case among savages, where a hatchet is given to obtain a pig, and a nail for a bunch of bananas.

When exchanges multiplied, while at the same time occupations were specialised, recourse was had to money; and barter was carried on by the double process of selling and buying.

In the *Iliad* (Bk vii. l. 472), when the vessels of Lemnos bring wine to the Greeks, "Then the long-haired Achæan bought them wine, some with bronze some with shining iron, some with skins, others with live oxen, others with slaves." Here we have primitive barter.

§ 2. Employment of Money: Sale and Purchase.

Aristotle first, and afterwards the Roman jurisconsult Paulus, have shown to perfection the origin and the function of money. This is how the Greek philosopher expresses himself:—

"The use of a currency was an indispensable device. People agreed mutually to give and receive some article, which, while it was in itself a commodity, was easy to handle in the business of life, some such article as iron or silver which was at first defined simply by size and weight, although finally they set a stamp upon every coin as a mark of its value to relieve themselves from the trouble of weighing it. Money, however, is in itself mere trash, having only a current or conventional, and not in any sense a natural value, because if the people by whom it is used give it up and adopt another, it is wholly valueless, and does not serve to supply any want" (Aristotle, *Politics*, i. vi., Welldon's translation).

The jurisconsult Paulus reproduces the same idea, but with greater precision:

" The origin of sale and purchase is found in barter. Money was unknown, and there were no words to distinguish the merchandise and the price; according to the needs and circumstances of the moment, every one bartered what he found useless for what was useful, for it often happens that one person has in excess that which another lacks. As, however, it did not always, nor easily happen, that when A had what B wanted, B in his turn had something that A was willing to accept, a substance was chosen whose value, being legal and constant, obviated the difficulties of barter by the equality of its quantity. This substance, marked with an official stamp, derives its usage and power of payment not from what it is composed of, but from its quantity. Henceforth the two objects exchanged are no longer both called *merchandise,* but one system only, while the other is called *price."*

Isidore of Seville (*Orig.* xvi. 17) sums up the doctrine of antiquity in these terms : "There are three things essential in money ; the substance, the law, and the form. In the absence of any one of these, money ceases to exist."

The final result of selling and buying is the barter of commodities either for other commodities or for services. I need food, clothing, and the services of the doctor, the lawyer, the judge, or the professor. In exchange I am able to offer the objects which I produce or the services which I can render. Barter takes place, and the needs on both sides are satisfied.

At bottom, the circulation of wealth effected by money or its substitutes, amounts to a series of barters, which the Roman law defines thus :—

(1). *Do ut des.* "Gift for gift," *e.g.* coin for wine.

(2). *Do ut facias.* "Gift for service," gold for the instruction of a son.

(3). *Facio ut des.* "Service for gift," work for food.

(4). *Facio ut facias.* "Service for service," the pleading a case for the making a coat.

§ 3. Influence of Exchange on Prosperity.

Exchange contributes enormously to the increase of wealth: in the first place indirectly by permitting specialisation and the division of labour of which we have pointed out the marvellous effects; in the second place directly, for it increases the utility of commodities by causing each object to reach the hands of the person to whom it can be most useful. Thus a farmer has a horse too slight to labour; a country doctor possesses one too heavy to go his rounds. They exchange. The farmer ploughs his furrows more easily, and the doctor pays his visits more quickly. Each is better suited and gains by the bargain; and so wealth is increased.

In primitive times each cluster of families produced nearly everything it consumed. Nowadays exchanges are incessantly made, between trade and trade, between country and town, between province and province; land and land, continent and continent. The poorest workman consumes the products of two hemispheres. The wool for his clothes comes from

Australia; the rice for his pudding from the Indies,
the corn for his bread from Illinois; the petroleum
for his lamp from Pennsylvania ; his coffee from Java ;
the cotton for his wife's dress from Egypt or Alabama ;
his knife from Sheffield ; the silk of his neck-tie from
France.

With each improvement in the means of communication, and the mechanism of circulation, there is
an increase in the number of exchanges.   It may
thus be said that the progress of economic civilisation
is measured by the progress of exchange.

CHAPTER II.

SALE AND PURCHASE.

§ 1. Price.

PRICE, in the broadest meaning of the term, is anything which is obtained in exchange for an object.
In its usual meaning it is the amount of money which
the exchange procures.

A thing's price is fixed by the competition established between those who wish to sell and those who
desire to buy it, that is to say by what is called " *the
law of demand and supply.*"

The supply of an article is the whole quantity
which there is a desire to sell; the demand, the
whole quantity which there is a desire to purchase

accompanied by ability to pay. When the supply exceeds the demand, prices fall; when the demand exceeds the supply, prices rise. Much cattle in the market and few buyers, prices fall; little cattle and many buyers, prices rise.

§ 2. Supply and Demand, and the Cost of Production.

The demand for an object is determined by the need for it, or, which comes to the same thing, by the utility of the object for satisfying a need. The supply depends on the abundance or rarity of the object of demand. An object is rare, either because it is difficult or costly to produce, as in the case of a chronometer, or, as in that of the diamond, because nature produces it only in small quantities.

The demand for corn is very strong, since it answers to a need of the first importance. Corn, however, is not dear, because the supply of it is always abundant, owing to the fact that it is not costly to produce. If, however, the supply fails, as it does in a besieged town, people will give everything to obtain corn. It follows that a slight falling off in the crop suffices to cause a great increase in price. This shows that the supply of commodities which can be produced at will depends on the cost of production.

The sum required to cover the expenses or cost of production has been called the "necessary" or "natural" price, and for this reason :—If the current price falls below this necessary price, the producer, finding himself a loser, ceases to produce it; the commodity becomes more rare, and, as a result, prices rise till they cover the expenses of production. On the other hand, if the current price rises above the cost of production, the exceptional profit of the manufacture attracts fresh capital, and by the increased production prices are made to fall. The current price is some-times above, sometimes below, the necessary price, but always tends to approach it.

For articles of which the quantity cannot be increased at will a monopoly price is established, which depends solely on the demand. The value of a picture is the price which the competition of picture buyers will force the most eager of them to give; and this because no one can now produce a picture of Rubens at any price.

For objects which can be multiplied, but at an ever-increasing expense, the necessary price will be equal to the outlay on that portion of those objects which shall have cost most to produce. If this outlay were not covered by the selling price, the objects would cease to be made. Let us suppose that the cost of production of coal in some mines is four shillings the ton, and in others seven shillings, the necessary price will be at least seven shillings. Since, if recourse must be had to the less abundant mines owing to the inability of the others to satisfy the demand, it is necessary that the selling price rise sufficiently high to defray the cost of production of this more hardly won coal. The same is the case

with corn, and with everything else which can only
be produced in greater quantities at a greater expense.
Thus, as we have already seen, the most favoured
productive agents, since their produce sells at the
same price while the expenses have been less,
confer exceptional advantages which give rise to
rent.

§ 3. The Just Price.

In ancient times, and in the Middle Ages, people
talked of a just price, *justum pretium*, that is to say,
of a price proportionate to the value of the object.
The only equitable basis of exchange must be the
equality of value of the objects exchanged.   If for
4*l.* I give a heifer worth 8*l.* I lose by the bargain,
and whoever buys the heifer is enriched at my
expense.   When the loss incurred exceeded half the
value, the Roman law permitted the sale to be re-
scinded, and the French code has sanctioned the same
principle.   Plato condemns those who try to sell corn
at more than its value, by concealing the fact of a ship's
arrival which will diminish its price, and St. Augus-
tin blames those whose only thought is to sell
dear and buy cheap, *vili velle emere et caro vendidere*
(*De Trinit.* xiii. 3).

Modern economists do not admit the conception of
a *just price.*   According to them the price accepted
by the two parties is always just.   The reason of
this is that they derive justice from convention, while
in reality convention must conform itself to justice.

From this latter principle result the maxims of practical uprightness which are accepted by all honest
tradesmen ; it is always a duty to " give good money's
worth," and to refrain from indulgence in deceit as to
the quality of goods.

§ 4. Usefulness of Fairs and Exchanges.

Since price is the result of the relation established
between the demand and the supply, the best way of
fixing prices is to put all those who respectively
supply and demand into communication. This is
the function of fairs and exchanges. Individually I
have no means of knowing how much I can obtain
for the sack of barley I have just harvested ; hence
isolated sales are accompanied by endless argument.
When once, however, all who wish to sell their corn
and all who wish to buy it, meet in one place ; out
of their competition will immediately result a current price, and enormous transactions will then be
easily effected in a few minutes.

Exchanges and fairs are thus institutions which
have as their aim and result the better application
of the law of demand and supply.

CHAPTER III.

MONEY.

§ 1. Nature and Function of Money.

MONEY is the substance or substances which custom or the law causes to be employed as the means of payment, the instrument of exchange, and the common measure of values.

The jurisconsult Paulus has shown us how the difficulty of bartering wares against wares caused the employment in exchanges of an intermediary as a means of purchase and payment. Money is thus the agent of circulation and the vehicle of exchange. It causes the property in an object to pass from one person to another, in the same way as a cart transports an object from one place to another.

As an American economist, Dana Horton (*Money and Law*, p. 14) has noted, from the first origin of barbarous societies, law or custom established tributes, fines, compositions, and forced gifts, and determined by means of what objects they should be paid. Money is thus a legal means of payment.

Money is at the same time the universal equivalent. When I sell goods for twenty shillings, the sovereign I receive is the equivalent of the goods I deliver, and by means of the sovereign of money I can, in my turn, obtain an equal value in commodities. "A piece of gold," says Adam Smith, "may be considered as an agreement for a certain quantity of goods payable by the tradesmen of the neighbourhood."

Lastly, money is a common measure or standard of values. It is difficult to compare the relative value of objects directly—to fix, for instance, the amount of corn which a sheep is worth. But the comparative valuation becomes easy by the employment in money of a common valuer. In the same way the length of objects is compared by means of the foot, the standard of long measure, and their heaviness by means of the pound, the standard of weight. Only the substance by means of which the comparative value of different articles of commerce is measured being itself merchandise delivered in exchange, its value varies like that of all goods. There is not, therefore, a fixed standard of values in the same way as there is of length and weight. What is desirable is to adopt one as fixed as possible.

Money, by its very constant and widely-admitted value, permits the accumulation of wealth and its transference from one country and generation to another. It is thus a means of conservation and transmission of wealth in time and space.

It is thanks to money that the division of labour and interdependence of the different trades and functions have been established. Money is thus the bond of human society.

§ 2. Different Kinds of Money.

Objects of every sort have been employed as money: in Siberia, furs; in Africa, cubes of salt, tickets of blue cotton, and cowrie-shells; iron at Sparta; and, in former times, almost universally, heads of cattle.

In the *Rig-Veda*, in the *Zend-Avesta*, and in Homer, objects are valued at so many head of cattle. The arms of Diomede are worth nine oxen, and those of Glaucos one hundred (*Iliad*, vi. 234). The tripod given as a prize to the wrestlers in the twenty-third book of the *Iliad* is valued at a dozen oxen, and a slave, a quick workwoman, at four (Gladstone, *Juventus Mundi*, p. 534). The tribute which the Frank conquerors imposed on the Saxons was reckoned in oxen. Our word " pecuniary " (*pecunia*) comes from *pecus*, "cattle," as does the legal term *peculium*.[1] The English word " fee " (Saxon, *feoh* = cattle) signifies " payment;" the Scandinavian *fä*, " wealth," is identical with it. The Greek word κτῆμα signifies both " property " and a " flock;" the Gothic *skatts*, " treasure" and "flock;" *schatz* in German, " treasure;" *Sket* in Frisian, " cattle." In Hebrew, *kassaph* means both " sheep" and " money;" *gamal*, " camel " and " payment;" *miknêh*, from the

---

[1] "Is it not strange," says the commentator **Festus**, " that these commonly used words are derived from cattle? Among the ancients it was of cattle that wealth and patrimonies chiefly consisted, so that we still speak of *pecunia, peculium*."

root *kana*, "to create," a "flock and an acquisition," or "price." The Sanskrit *rupya*, the rupee of Indian coinage, is derived from *rûpa*, "cattle."

Metal money was at first employed as representing money in cattle, for a passage in the *Agamemnon* of Æschylus seems to show that the ancient Greek pieces of money used to bear the mark of an ox, and the same was the case with the Roman *as*.

When, with the progress of civilisation, exchanges had become more frequent, moneys were made exclusively of gold or silver. The simultaneous and universal employment of these two metals is due to their possessing, in a greater degree than any other substance, the qualities which a good money ought to unite. These qualities are as follow :—

(1) Gold and silver do not in the least deteriorate with keeping. Minted, melted down, and re-minted, the gold gathered by the Greeks and Romans, in part, still circulates among us.

(2) The production of the precious metals is restrained by the scarcity of the ores. As a result they have great value in proportion to their weight, and this facilitates their handling, transport, and hoarding.

(3) Augmented by annual production, diminished by accidental losses and wear and tear, the sum of the precious metals throughout the world, of which the value in money and ornaments is valued at about 2,000,000,000*l.*, increases slowly, and in nearly the same proportion as the increase of the need for money

which arises from the development of population and of the total amount of the exchanges in the world. The demand and supply being thus nearly at an equilibrium, the value of gold and silver is very stable.

(4) This immense stock of the precious metals lessens the variations in value which might result from the variations in the annual supply; just as the level of a great lake is little affected by any changes in the discharge of the rivers which flow into it.

(5) The precious metals are sought after and accepted everywhere, an indispensable condition for an object to be a general medium of exchange. They are received in every civilised country, and can thus serve as a means of universal payment.

(6) They are easily divisible, and each part has a value proportionate to its weight.

(7) They receive and preserve unaltered the imprint which makes known their origin and nominal value, and thus also their weight in pure metal.

(8) They are easily recognisable: gold by its weight, silver by its sound.

Of all these qualities of money the most essential is that of stability of value; inasmuch as a change in its value affects all contracts.

§ 3. Value of Money.

The value of money is measured by the quantity of objects it procures, that is to say, by its power of purchase.

O

In the Middle Ages three bushels of corn could be bought for the pure silver contained in five of our shillings. Nowadays only a fourth as much could be obtained for the money. Silver, therefore, is worth only the fourth of what it was before the discovery of America.

The value of the precious metals has diminished to this extent, despite the enormous increase in their employment, because their sum total and annual production have been considerably augmented. The sum total of gold and silver existing in Europe in the year 1500 is estimated at 80,000,000*l.*, and the annual production at about 1,000,000*l.* The present sum total in the whole world must now be over 2,000,000,000*l.*, and the annual production about 36,000,000*l.*

The value of money, like that of any other object, depends on the relation between the supply and demand. The supply is the result of the quantity of money in circulation and the rapidity with which it circulates. If every shilling effects three purchases in a day, to accomplish the same number of exchanges three times fewer shillings will be needed than if each shilling only changed hands once. The supply and usefulness of the same amount of money are thus trebled. The demand for money is the result of the number of changes which have to be effected by means of cash. If the supply of money increases beyond the demand, its value decreases and prices rise. If the demand, *i.e.* the number of exchanges requiring payment in cash, increases beyond the amount of money in circulation, the value of money rises and prices fall. Lastly, if the quantity of money and number of exchanges increase equally, but at the same time means are found for effecting certain transactions without having recourse to cash, the employment of this is diminished, its supply increases, and prices rise.

Gold and silver ornaments affect prices as creating a demand for money, not as supplying it; for cash is needed in buying and selling these ornaments. The precious metals, again, in the form of ingots, only affect prices when they are represented by bills which fulfil the functions of money. Lastly, the cost of production of the precious metals only affects their value in proportion as it contributes to modify their quantity and in consequence, the supply.

§ 4. Is the Abundance of Money an Advantage ?

It is no advantage for mankind in general, or for an isolated country, to possess much money ; as many exchanges can be effected with little money as with much. Prices diminish in proportion to the falling off in the quantity of cash, and the rarer and more valuable the unit of money becomes the more exchanges will it effect. If mankind possessed twice as much money as at present, it would be none the richer. It would have no greater number of commodities or means of enjoyment. Every one's situation would remain as it was before. Everything

o 2

else would be the same, but prices would be doubled.
Two shillings would be paid where one was paid
before, and the money value of all goods would be
twice as high—a change advantageous to nobody.

An alteration, however, in the value of money,
while in course of accomplishment, brings great
confusion into all legal and economic relations,
inasmuch as all debts and contracts are based on the
prices which are changing. The farmer who owes
the state twenty shillings for taxes and the holder
of a mortgage a like sum for interest, when the
quarter of wheat sells for forty shillings, pays these
two debts with the price of a single quarter. If
money, and, consequently, prices diminish by one-
half, to pay his debts he will have to surrender two
quarters of his wheat instead of one.

A decrease in the stock of money, whether absolute
or relative, by lowering prices, has as its immediate
consequence the restriction both of exchanges and
production. Its final result is a heavy burden upon
debtors.

An increase in the amount of money, by raising
prices, stimulates exchanges and production and
relieves debtors. Hence the discovery of America
by Christopher Columbus, and of the gold fields of
California in 1848, may be said with truth to have
saved many a bankruptcy.

It is desirable that the value of money should
remain as stable as possible, and this will be the case
so long as its quantity increases in the same pro-

portion as the number of exchanges for which cash is required.

§ 5. Monetary Systems.

In primitive times the precious metals were used as a means of exchange by being weighed, and this is still the case in China and many other countries. With the Romans the As was originally the unit both of weight and of money. In England the pound is the monetary unit and the unit of weight. The French monetary system is derived from that of Charlemagne, in which the unit was the *livre* or pound of silver. In order to facilitate the use of gold and silver the state then struck pieces of them on which were specified their weight, the amount of pure metal they contained, their name, and, consequently, their legal value or power of payment. Thus, in order to pay a sum of money, it is no longer necessary to assay and weigh the metal, but only to count over a certain number of coins.

To make the pieces of gold and silver hard, and thus less liable to wear, a certain proportion of copper is added to the pure metal ; this is called the *alloy.* The proportion between the pure metal and the alloy is the standard which, in the English sovereign, is eleven parts of pure metal to one of alloy. A coin is said to be good money when it is of the legal standard.

The unit of money is the coin of gold or silver

of which the other coins are the multiples or measures. In England this is the sovereign; in France, the franc; in Germany, the mark; in Holland, the florin; and in the United States, the dollar. Among coins there are some which have a legal currency for all payments without limit; others, of an inferior quality, have only legal currency for small payments; while, for the smallest payments of all, "token money" is issued, generally made of bronze or nickel. In England "coppers" may be tendered up to the value of a shilling, and silver to that of 2l.

The sum of the laws and regulations concerning money constitutes the monetary system.

Formerly all sovereign powers—monarchs, cities, bishops, and lords—reserved to themselves the right of coining money, because by issuing it at a nominal value greater than that of the metal it contained they received the difference of these two values, called *seigneurage*, as their profit, and made it a source of revenue. At different periods they abused their right of coinage to diminish the value of the currency, either by lessening the amount of pure metal contained in the coins, or by increasing their legal value. If, by adding more alloy, two coins are struck from the pure metal which formerly made one, or if it be proclaimed that a coin be received at double its former value, all payments are halved. This was the way that bankrupt states formerly made composition. Thus, a French king, Philippe le

Bel, nicknamed the Coiner, because he made great use of false coining to diminish his debts, is placed by Dante in Hell,—

> La si vedrà il duol che sopra Senna
> Induce, falseggiando la moneta
> Quei che morrà di colpo di cotenna.
>   (*Parad.* xix. 118—120.)

"There will be seen the misery caused on the banks of Seine through the falsifying of money by him who is to die from the blow of a wild boar."

Plutarch relates that for the relief of debtors Solon decreed that the mina should in future be worth a hundred drachmas instead of seventy-three, and adds: "In this way, by paying apparently the full value, though really less, those who owed large sums gained considerably, without causing any loss to their creditors." He here expresses the error which has inspired all the issues of "depreciated" and paper money. No one seems to lose because payments are made just as well with coins reduced in value as with the unreduced. What is forgotten is that prices rise in proportion as the unit of money loses its value.

The best instance of this reduction in value, owing to the successive "diminutions" decreed by different sovereigns, is afforded by the French coinage in which the livre which, as issued by Charlemagne, was a pound's weight of silver and worth about fifty two shillings, by the end of the eighteenth century had a value of no more than ninepence halfpenny. In

England the £ has lost not quite two-thirds of its primitive value.

In order thoroughly to understand historical passages where sums of money and prices are concerned, it is necessary to know, firstly, what quantity of gold and silver these sums represented in the period in question; and, secondly, what quantity of goods could be obtained for a certain weight of the precious metal. Thus in Greece, in the time of Solon, the drachma was worth something over ninepence, and was the price of a medimnus, or about twelve gallons, of wheat. In Rome the Papirian law *De multarum æstimatione* (B.C. 430), which converted the old fines of cattle into sums of money, fixed the value of a sheep at ten *asses*, and that of a bullock at one hundred. As the *as libralis*, composed of an alloy of copper, tin, and lead, was worth about fivepence farthing, the price of a sheep was thus about four shillings and sixpence, and that of a bullock about forty-four shillings.

At the present time, in civilised countries, the coining of standard money is free. Any one has the right to take an unlimited amount of ore to the mint, and to receive in exchange an equal weight of current coin, with a deduction for the expenses of fabrication or coining, and in England without any deduction at all. It is thus private persons who cause money to be coined, but in conformance with a legal tariff. According to this tariff, 3*l*. 11*s*. 10½*d*. is paid in England for each ounce of gold of a fineness of eleven-twelfths. In France and in the Latin Union where, however, free coinage is at present suspended, 3,100 francs are given for a kilogramme of gold of a fineness of nineteenths, and 200 francs for a kilogramme of silver of the same standard.

The right of coining the inferior money the state reserves to itself for two reasons: because its intrinsic value is less than its nominal, and because, the legal currency being limited, only a limited quantity is required. The free coinage of money in the two metals was introduced into England in 1666, and in France by the " loi du 7 germinal an xi." (1803).

The monetary system flourishing in the countries which in 1863 formed the Latin Monetary Union (France, Italy, Switzerland, and Belgium) admits as standard money all gold coins and five-franc pieces. Other silver coins are of an inferior standard, of a fineness of only 835 parts in 1,000. These have only legal currency in each payment up to the amount of fifty francs, and the associated states cannot issue more than six francs for each inhabitant.

Token money in France and Italy is made of bronze, in Switzerland and Belgium of nickel. It serves for very small payments, and no more than five francs of it need be accepted. In England copper money is only current to the amount of a shilling.

An excellent provision in the Latin Union is a

stipulation by which inferior coins and token money
can be changed at the public banks for standard
coins, when offered for a sum fixed by law.   In this
way the amount of small money can never become too
great, since any unnecessary surplus can be converted
into standard money.

§ 6. Monometallism and Bimetallism.

The monetary system of the Latin Union is called
the "double-standard or bimetallic system," because
it permits, in principle, the free and unlimited
coinage both of gold and silver pieces, to each of which
it gives legal currency, *i.e.*, the right to be accepted in
all payments, every debt being presumed in law to
be payable in coins having a legal currency.

The monometallic system only accords free coinage
and unlimited legal currency to pieces of one metal,
either gold, as in England, or silver, as in Austria.
This system seems the simpler of the two, and fixes
more exactly the relations of value between the
different pieces of standard money, since these are
all made of the same metal.   The relation of value,
however, between money and the goods of which
it has to effect the exchange is more variable with
a monometallic system than with a bimetallic.
Just as a compensated pendulum, with its bars
made of two metals of unequal expansiveness, is
less liable to variation because their inequalities
balance; or just as a river with two tributaries flows
more regularly than it would with only one, so a

monetary system, fed by the simultaneous influx of both precious metals, is rendered more stable, because the total mass of standard money is greater, and because a falling off in the production of one of the two metals may be compensated by an increase in the production of the other.

§ 7. The Laws of Gresham and Newton.

A great drawback in the bimetallic system is expressed in what is called Gresham's law. Sir Thomas Gresham, one of the councillors of Queen Elizabeth, showed in 1558 that the money which has the less value always ousts that which has the greater from circulation, this last being exported. Aristophanes (*Frogs*, l. 718) has recorded the same observation: "In our state," he says, "the bad citizens are preferred to the good, just as bad money circulates while the good is hoarded."

In 1717 Newton first indicated the means of obviating the vexatious effect of Gresham's law, by establishing the relation of value between gold and silver the same in all countries; pointing out that, if this were done, there would no longer be any motive for exporting one of the two metals in preference to the other. The economic law thus formulated by the great discoverer of gravitation, should serve as a basis for a monetary union between all civilised states, which should draw closer the ties and relations between the associated nations.

Till quite modern times silver has always been

employed as the chief kind of money. In French
the word *argent* is used as a synonym for money, and
siller in Scotland had long a similar meaning. Silver
is in fact the better metal for monetary use, since its
value is more stable than that of gold, and this is the
essential quality for the legal medium of payments,
and the common measure of values. The value of
silver is more stable than that of gold because it is
exclusively obtained from the working of mines. The
production of gold, three-fourths of which is obtained
from auriferous sands, increases and diminishes, as
history shows, in a very short time. If gold were
everywhere adopted as the sole standard metal, prices
would be subject to numerous and abrupt fluctuations,
and this is a great evil.

§ 8. The Maintenance of Monetary Systems.

To maintain a monetary system in its integrity
the following legislative measures are indispensable.

(1) The making and issuing false money, or
counterfeiting or clipping the legal money, must be
prohibited and punished.

(2) A minimum weight must be fixed which coins
must possess or lose their legal currency and be liable
to be refused in payment.

(3) At the expense either of the state or the last
owner, all these coins of less than the minimum legal
weight must be withdrawn from circulation and
reminted. Since the coins have been worn by the

use of the public at large, and not of the last owner, it is juster for the expense of reminting to be borne by the state.

CHAPTER IV.

CREDIT.

§ 1. What Credit is.

CREDIT is the act of confidence by which the holders of a sum of money or a quantity of goods delivers them to another person on his promise of reimbursement or payment. The word credit comes from the Latin *credere*, " to believe." Whoever delivers to another person either money or goods on the condition that after a certain time they shall restore the sum lent, or pay the price agreed, does so because he *believes* that this promise will be fulfilled. The person who credits this promise and has the right to demand payment is the *creditor*. The person who promises and is under an obligation to pay is the *debtor*. The sum which has to be paid is called a *debt*, and is said to be placed to the *credit* of the first and the *debit* of the second. The time which has to run till the moment of payment is the *term*.

Promise and confidence in a promise, these, then, are the elements of credit. That which inspires confidence is solvency, intelligence, the spirit of order and uprightness. Laws which develop these qualities and insure the rigorous execution of engagements have as their result the expansion and increase of credit—a good instance of the way in which virtues and just laws favour the production of wealth.

A debt when acknowledged in writing gives rise to different kinds of vouchers, bank notes, bills payable to order, letters of exchange, cheques, bills of sale, municipal and joint stock debentures, and state loans.

"Personal" credit has as its basis either the individual qualities or the fortune, real or supposed, of the debtor. "Real" credit depends on the goods (*res*) which he pledges or gives as security. "Real" pledges are more trustworthy than personal security. *Plus est cautionis in re quam in persona* is the expression of that "stereotype of good sense" the Roman laws.

§ 2. The Advantages and Effects of Credit.

Credit fosters the productivity of labour and enables it to increase wealth; it does not however increase wealth itself. In other words, it augments the activity of capital, not its quantity. All credit is summed up in a promise or an order to pay, *i.e.* in a signature; and capital cannot be created by a stroke of the pen.

Credit seems to multiply capital because side by side with the thing owed appears the promise which confers a right to it. In reality, however, these are not two separate things; one is only the shadow of the other. Burn every I O U in the world, and nothing real will have ceased to exist. Only the legal relations have been changed, since the creditors lose exactly what the debtors gain. When a house is reflected in the water, it may be said that there are two houses. The water ruffles, and the reflection vanishes; but the real house continues to exist. When I buy a promise to pay a hundred pounds, what I acquire is the future possession of this sum with the interest attached to it. Wealth, and a title to possess this wealth, cannot be reckoned as two things.

The following are some of the useful effects of credit.

(1) Credit brings to labour the capital necessary for production.

A man with strong arms takes possession of a piece of fertile land : he lacks, however, the tools to cultivate it and provisions to maintain him until harvest-time; for lack of these he dies of hunger and the land remains unproductive. Instead of this, suppose I lend him the means of procuring tools and subsistence : he sets to work, and at the end of the year repays me my advance; henceforth he can live on the fruits of his labour. This is an instance of how credit favours the increase of wealth by coming to the aid of labour.

(2) Credit puts savings in motion and thus prevents capital lying unemployed.

In the East no one dares to lend his savings for

fear of losing them. He prefers to convert them into
jewels with which he ornaments his chibouque, his
yataghan, or the harness of his horse. Perhaps, more
prudent still, he buries them in order that they may
escape the greed of the government. Thus the wealth
which his savings creates in no way furthers production.
Credit has no existence. On the other hand, in
Scotland, landlords, farmers, manufacturers, artisans,
all deposit their disposable funds in banks, by which
they are immediately advanced to producers. In
this way no article of capital is left unemployed.
Founded on honesty and the love of work, credit
reigns and accomplishes marvels.

(3) Credit brings capital into the hands of those
who will make the best use of it.

New capital is for the most part created by persons
unoccupied in any industry and thus unable to
employ it remuneratively. The means of drawing an
income from it is to lend it, either directly, or through
the medium of a banker, to those who will pay most
for the use of it, *i.e.* to those who will employ
it most productively. Credit is thus constantly
transferring capital to the places and hands in which
it brings in the most. As a consequence it affords an
incentive to saving by assuring to thrift a reward, not
only immediate, but as high as can be paid.

(4) Credit allows of the immediate execution of
great works, or of the meeting of extraordinary
needs, such as those which arise in time of war, by
discounting the revenues or produce expected in the

future. Even in this case, however, it must not be supposed that credit *creates* anything; it only determines the disposition of capital already in existence.

There is no such thing, as some assert, as anticipating the future, or releasing capital once invested. We can only use what is actually in existence at the given moment. The expressions quoted are metaphorical; and in political economy, as elsewhere, metaphors are dangerous weapons to handle.

(5) Credit creates economical methods of payment.

In this way it allows exchanges to be made with a smaller quantity of metallic money. Gold and silver are set free, and can be devoted to industry, or exported in exchange for objects useful either for consumption or production. As Adam Smith has said, credit opens for the exchange of productions paths through the air, and thus the ordinary roads can be put under cultivation, and increase the production of articles of food. This advantage, however, is, in part, more apparent than real. The gold and silver remain in the country, or if we take the world at large as our field of observation, the addition of bills to the means of exchange afforded by metallic money, tends towards a rise of prices. On the other hand, it is no less certain that the greater facility of exchange will give a stimulus to industry and commerce, which will then, in their turn, require more of the instruments

of exchange.   When this is the case there will be no
depreciation of money, nor rise of prices.

The way in which credit performs the functions of
money is as follows :   A solvent person promises to
pay 50*l.* ; this promise, in which implicit confidence
is placed, is received in payment as readily as fifty
sovereigns, and, as it passes from hand to hand,
influences all transactions in the same way as they
would be influenced by these sovereigns to which it
gives a title, and represents.   Side by side with the
circulation resting on coin, there is thus established
a circulation resting on confidence, the instruments
of which possess the following advantages :

(1) They are less cumbrous than the precious
metals.

(2) They enable large sums to be counted more
easily.

(3) They are not exposed to the wear and tear,
which gradually lessens the weight of coins.

(4) They can be more easily sent to a distance.

(5) Some of them can be so constructed that
their unlawful possessor can obtain no payment.

All the instruments of credit rest on a basis of
metal money, since they confer a right to receive a
sum in coin.   But, in so far as they circulate, they
fulfil the functions of money.

§ 3. The Drawbacks of Credit.

The mother says to her son, " Buy nothing except
for money ; credit is ruinous."   The father tells him,

"Credit is the soul of industry; it is the refusal of it that ruins." Both are right : the mother who speaks of the poisonous credit that ministers to unproductive consumption, the father who alludes to the beneficent credit that forwards production. Unfortunately the borrowers on the largest scale, *i.e.* Governments, have recourse more often to the first kind of credit than to the second, and devour capital unproductively in war and the preparations for war.

Credit, also, by permitting purchases from funds which people hope to, not only which they do, possess, favours hazardous speculations and the over excitement of industry and commerce.

§ 4. The Instruments of Credit.

All instruments of credit are alike in consisting of a voucher which affirms the rights of the creditors with respect to a debtor.

(1) In the *acknowledgement*, A acknowledges himself indebted to B in the sum of 50*l.* and promises to pay the same.

(2) In the *bill payable to bearer at sight*, A promises to pay 50*l.* to any person who shall present the bill, and at the moment of presentation; this is the bank-note. The bank-note when accepted in payment extinguishes the debt the same as money does, and thus, to the extent that it is received, performs the function of the latter.

(3) In the *bill to order*, A has purchased goods to

the value of 50*l.* from B, and, instead of paying ready money, gives him a bill in these terms :—

I promise to pay to B, or his order, the sum of 50l., payable July 1st, 1882.

This bill is transferable, so that if B owes 50*l.* to C, he can pay it, with C's consent, by passing him on the bill signed by A and *endorsing* it, *i.e.* writing on the back, " Pay to C or to his order." Each time that a bill thus endorsed passes from one person to another, it effects a provisional payment, which does not become final unless the bill is paid on its expiry. On the day of expiry, the last holder has to present the bill to the original debtor who created it. If the debtor fail to pay, his refusal must be established, at the latest the second day after the expiry, by an act called a *protest.* If this protest is duly made, the successive endorsers of the bill are severally bound to make it good, until the first creditor, B, (the *drawer*) is reached, on whom falls the loss resulting from A's inability to pay.

(4) The *bill of exchange* is created and afterwards transmitted by endorsement in exactly the same way as the bill to order, from which it differs only in its form. Instead of the debtor who promises to pay, it is now the creditor who gives the debtor an order to pay, thus :

London, July 1st, 1883.

At three months pay to the order of C the sum of 50l.

To M B, Brussels   *Signed*   A
    (*The debtor*).   (*The creditor*).

The great advantage of the bill of exchange is that, when *drawn* from one place on another, it settles the reciprocal debts of these places, and dispenses with the transmission of coin. For example living in London I have to pay 50*l.* to M. Pierre at Paris. Mr. Smith, on the other hand, has 50*l.* to receive from a M. Jacques at Paris, and draws a bill on him for this sum. I buy this bill of Smith, who is thus paid, and send it to my creditor, M. Pierre. M. Pierre presents the bill to M. Jacques, and when the latter has paid it, M. Pierre's claim on me is also satisfied. Both debts have thus been paid, and no money has been sent from one city to another. Exchanges between country and country are regulated in the same manner, almost entirely without the transmission of coin. English merchants pay for their purchases in France by transmitting bills drawn by Englishmen on Frenchmen.

(5) A *cheque* is an order to pay at sight a certain sum to the credit of the bearer. When several persons have the same banker, payments from one to another can be made by cheques and *transfers of account* in the simplest possible manner. Thus if I owe Smith 50*l.*, I send him a cheque on our common banker, with whom we both have a current account. The banker subtracts 50*l.* from my *balance, i.e.* the amount due to me, and carries it to Smith's. This transfer, made in two lines of writing, suffices to effect the payment. The Bank of France effects these settlements of its clients' reciprocal debts to

the amount of more than 1,600,000,000*l.* In London and New York clerks from the principal banks meet every day in the "Clearing House," and there balance the cheques they hold against each other. These balancings amount in the course of the year, in London to about 5,000,000,000*l.*, and in New York to rather over a thousand millions more.

(6) *Warrants and certificates of bonding.* Warrants certifying that goods have been bonded in a public warehouse or dock, can be used for giving a creditor security, but not as a means of payment. On the other hand certificates of the warehousing of coin, or even of gold and silver ingots, serve perfectly as a means of paying the sum which they represent.

(7) *Mortgage bonds* are bonds representing a fraction of the mortgages possessed by the bank which issues them on the property of the debtor. They confer a right to interest and repayment in an order determined by lot. The raiser of the mortgage pays interest, and an annual sum which is devoted to the extinction of the debt by a certain time.

(8) *Debentures* are bonds representing debts contracted by industrial companies, chiefly railways. They give a right to interest, paid yearly or half yearly, and to repayment, often with a premium, in an order determined by lot.

(9) *Municipal debentures* represent the debts of various cities. Frequently they are in similar terms to the bonds just mentioned.

(10) *Government stocks* represent the debts owed
by the various Governments as a result of their
loans. In general, Governments engage to pay a
certain interest, not to refund the capital at any
fixed date, whence the term, *"perpetual or con-
solidated debt."* States which have the means
gradually refund their debts, by the operation of
a *sinking fund*, buying bonds on the Stock Exchange,
and destroying them.

Bonds of the description of numbers 7, 8, 9, and
10, representing loans for long terms, cannot serve
in the place of money. The other bonds do so to a
certain extent, but the only perfect substitute for coin
is the bank-note with its power of effecting a final
payment.

Money in the shape of bills was employed at
Carthage. In a dialogue entitled " Eryxias Æschinè,"
Socraticus, in a discussion on the nature of wealth,
relates how " The Carthaginians provide themselves
with money in the following manner. In a small
piece of leather there is sewn an object of the size of
a stater (a Greek coin), but only those who have made
the seam know what this object is. A mark is then
stamped upon the leather, and henceforth it is used
as money. Those persons are considered the wealthiest
who have the most of these objects, though among us
they would be of no more value than the pebbles of
our mountains." This quotation explains the whole
mystery of the circulation of credit. Objects of a
limited quantity and receivable in all payments at a

value fixed by law, discharge to perfection the function of an equivalent sum of money, for this function consists in procuring the holder everything he desires up to the nominal value of these objects. Metal money has only this additional advantage of possessing also intrinsically as merchandise the conventional value attributed to it by law.

§ 5. Banks.

Banks are institutions which facilitate the operations of credit and the circulation of its instruments. Bankers and joint-stock banks must possess a capital of their own; but they work chiefly by receiving the capital of one set of persons to lend it in different manners to another. Their principal operations are as follow :—

(1) *The receipt of deposits.* Banks receive on deposit capital of which its proprietors are unable to make use, and lend it to persons in a position to employ it profitably. To do this, bankers must know the solvency of their borrowers. The bank's profit consists in the difference between the interest which it pays its depositors and that paid by its borrowers.

In countries where the employment of credit is well understood, every one who has daily to make payments, makes a deposit at his bankers, and pays by means of cheques on these deposits. In England bank deposits exceed 320,000,000*l.*, and in France 80,000,000*l.* In this way reciprocal debts are balanced and settled without resort to coin. The manner in which this is effected is as follows : Let us suppose that in a village every one has an account open at the same banker's. The farmer will then pay his rent by causing the amount to be written off his balance and transferred to his landlord's. The landlord in paying for the bread supplied to his house will transfer the price to the balance of the baker. The baker will pay the corn and flour dealer, and this latter the farmer who sells him his wheat, in the same manner. In this way products pass from hand to hand in the successive forms which labour gives them, from their first production till they are finally consumed. Property in the objects is transferred at the same time at each exchange, but without the employment of an equivalent in specie, as bills. The farmer's deposit or credit at the bank, by changing possessors, will have served to settle the successive transactions, apportioning to each the share he can claim in the value of the products. This simple example supplies the key to the marvellous machinery of credit as it is in operation in England and America.

(2) *The keeping open of current accounts.* The bank keeps an account open for each of its clients, with one column for the *credit* and another for the *debit.* All sums received are carried to the credit side, all sums paid on the client's account to the debit. Interest is due to the depositor or to the bank according to to whose advantage is the balance of credit when the debited are greater than those credited.

(3) *Discounting bills,* i.e. *promises to pay, bills to*

order, and bills of exchange. Any one who has sold
goods and received in payment either a promise or a
bill of exchange drawn on the debtor, may have
occasion to convert these bills into ready money
in order to discharge his own obligations for labour,
rent, or the purchase of provisions, &c. If the
banker puts trust in the solvency of the debtor and
creditor, the latter of whom by, his endorsement, is
also made responsible for the ultimate payment, he
takes over the bill, and gives its value after deducting
interest on the sum paid, calculated according to the
term to run before the bill expires, *i.e.* before the day
of payment, and also according to the current rate of
interest. This transaction is called " discounting"
and the rate of interest is called the " rate of discount."
Discounting really amounts to the purchase of the
credit represented by the bill. Discounting is the
principal operation of credit. Every fluctuation of
production and exchange depends on this, since
manufacturers and merchants ordinarily settle their
purchases by means of bills.

(4) *Issue of bank-notes.* In the year 807 the
Emperor of China, Hiang-Tsong, ordered that gold
and silver money should be deposited in the imperial
treasury, and in exchange for it gave certificates,
which circulated as legal currency, and were completely accepted as such by commerce. To these
certificates was given the very appropriate name of
fei-tsien, or " flying money." The Bank of Venice
(founded in 1171), the Banks of Amsterdam (1609),

of Hamburg (1629), and Rotterdam (1635), issued
certificates of deposit representing, in round figures,
the value in pure metal of the coin deposited in their
safes. These bills, which gave a right to a fixed
weight of gold or silver, were preferred, as a means
of payment, to the current coinage, the value of which
was often modified either by edict of the government
or by wear and tear. Bank-notes were at a premium,
and the use of them in payments was made a matter
of stipulation. At the present time this form of
credit-money is in general use in all civilised countries,
and has even often been misused.

As a means of payment, if not recognised by law,
at least universally accepted, bank-notes payable at
sight or to bearer, are used instead of bills of commerce,
which only circulate among persons who know each
other, and are of assured responsibility. These notes
are also usually preferred to metal money, as lighter,
and more convenient when large sums have to be
counted. In France, when after 1848 the issue of
notes was restricted to a maximum insufficient for
the needs of exchange, a premium was paid to obtain
them.

The value of the bank-notes issued is covered by
a fund in coin or ingots, and by discounted bills,
which together constitute the "reserve." It is estimated that a note-issuing bank ought to have in
cash one-third of its notes in circulation. A law
passed in 1844, called the Bank Charter Act, subjects
the Bank of England to a still more stringent rule.

By this law, every issue of notes in excess of fourteen and a half millions sterling, must be covered by an equal sum in legal money or ingots, so that the instrument of exchange can only increase in the proportion which it would observe if it were exclusively metal.

Prudence commands banks which issue notes to keep their reserve fund at a suitable level by raising the rate of discount when the precious metals are leaving the country.

In times of great crises, Governments sometimes decree a "forced currency." By this decree banks are authorised to refuse to make good their notes at sight, and all persons are obliged to receive these non-convertible notes in all payments at their nominal value. This extreme measure has as its object to enable banks sometimes to continue to lend their credit to commercial and industrial firms, which is a good thing ; sometimes to make advances to the State in the form of notes forced on the public, which is an evil, and one which becomes greater in proportion as the issue of these non-convertible notes is more considerable.

When the amount of these non-convertible notes surpasses the needs of the circulation, like everything else that is in excess, they depreciate in value. This depreciation takes the form of a general rise of prices. It can be exactly measured by comparing the value of the unit of money in paper, and that of the same unit in metal. Thus the Russian silver rouble is worth about three shillings and fourpence, while the paper rouble, at present, is only worth two and twopence. So in England in 1810, to obtain a gold guinea, in gold, or an equivalent weight of the metal, paper money had to be given of the nominal value of a guinea and a quarter.

Convertible notes are "money of paper," and this necessarily keeps on an equality with metal money, since the holder of a note, sooner than submit to a loss, will demand that it be redeemed. On the other hand, the non-convertible notes of a forced currency are "paper-money," and the depreciation of this is only limited in the same extent as is its issue in excess. The most memorable example of this depreciation is the case of the *assignats*. The French Republic had confiscated property of the clergy and emigrants to the value of over two hundred millions. To facilitate its sale, on the proposition of Mirabeau, the State issued notes called "assignats," because they were "assigned" for the purchase of the property of the nation. Since the lands purchased were to be paid for with these notes, which were to be destroyed on their return from circulation, with the sale of the last of the acres the last of the notes should have been cancelled.

The assignats remained at par to the end of 1792, though they had been issued to the amount of two thousand million livres, (80,000,000*l.*). To meet, however, the requirements of the war, they were created to the amount of forty-five thousand millions (1,800,000,000*l.*),

and their value diminished in proportion to the increase
of their issue.   During the summer of 1795, one
hundred livres in assignats were hardly worth one in
silver, and their value varied enormously from day to
day.   The price in assignats **of a pair of** boots was
fifteen hundred livres.   **In July, 1796,** their legal
currency was suppressed.   The important lesson
afforded by these **facts** is that credit-money, even
when guaranteed by real property, depreciates in
value if it is issued in excess of the requirements of
the circulation.

§ 6. Free Creation of Note-issuing Banks.

The issue of bank-notes should be permitted to all
persons and companies accepting responsibility for
their acts; but it should be prohibited to companies
with limited liability because these constitute an
exception to the principles of the common law.

The control of the currency has always, and rightly,
been recognised as an attribute of the State.   The
quantity of money in circulation has an influence on
all prices, and, as a consequence, on the financial
situation and the legal relations of every individual.
Bank-notes, however, are a money made of paper,
acting on prices just like money made of metal.   The
history of the banks of the United States shows
clearly the dangers of an unlimited power of issuing
these notes.

Progress has led us from local currency to national
currency, and from national currency to international

currency. The same progress must be made in the case of bank-notes. The unity of the means of exchange has the greatest advantages, and their diversity the greatest inconveniences.

CHAPTER V.

MONETARY, COMMERCIAL, AND INDUSTRIAL CRISES.

§ 1. Nature of Crises.

CRISES are the diseases of credit, for countries where credit is little used escape them. Sometimes they are as sharp as an inflammation, sometimes as slow and insidious as an anemic. They produce widespread disturbance in the money market, and consequently in production, and thus occasion heavy losses and numerous failures. Three varieties of crises may be distinguished, (1) monetary and commercial, (2) industrial, (3) speculative; and their phenomena demand as careful study as any in economy, since a knowledge of crises diminishes the risks of loss and increases the means of gain.

§ 2. The Periodical recurrence of Commercial and Monetary Crises.

For the last century, *i.e.* ever since the employment of credit became general in England, economic crises have occurred nearly every tenth year, the exact dates being 1763, 1783, 1793, 1803, 1825, 1838, 1847

1857, 1864 to 1866, 1875 to 1879.   It has been
thought that a kind of natural law may be observed
in this periodical character of this return.   Mr.
Jevons, who treats political economy mathematically,
has even suggested that crises are determined by the
spots in the sun.   Their principal cause, he says, is
the exportation of specie.   Specie is exported to pay
for the import of grain during years in which the
harvest is bad.   Bad harvests are the result of in-
clement summers, and these are caused by the spots
in the sun.   This explanation is ingenious, but has
the defect of being untrue to facts.   That crises
should recur periodically is not a natural law.   The
fact that they do so recur is explained by the re-
currence of the circumstances by which they are
produced ; and the science of finance can teach us
how to exorcise them.

§ 3. Characteristics of Crises.

Crises mostly occur at the end of several consecutive
years of prosperity, during which capital has been
accumulating.   This abundant supply of capital
lowers the rate of interest.   Cheap money stirs up
the spirit of enterprise.   Numerous companies are
started, and the bonds which represent their capital
are in great demand.   The rise in prices soon brings
in large profits to the bond-holders.   Every one is
anxious to buy, to gain a share in these profits; and
so the rise continues and stimulates the demand by
the increasing bonus which it brings in.   No one loses.

Everything that is touched turns to gold. The prices of commodities also rise, for the people who have grown rich increase their consumption. The period is one of "expansion," based on the employment of credit in all its forms. At last something happens which absorbs specie, the basis of credit; for example, an exceptional importation of grain induced by a poor harvest, or large investments in foreign securities. The bank which regulates the market raises the rate of discount. Credit contracts. Confidence disappears. Distrust spreads. A panic breaks out; every one wishes to sell, and no more buyers can be found. Prices fall lower and lower. Credit is absolutely refused, and we have reached the period of "revulsion." Deprived of the power both of borrowing and selling, those who have payments to make are involved in failure. One bankruptcy follows on another. A crisis has come.

This in its violence does not last long. The excessive fall in all prices once more attracts buyers, and money and credit return with them. To recover, however, from such disasters many years are needed, and these are called the period of "recovery." At the end of this the period of expansion recommences, to end in a fresh crisis, and so the circle begins again. This succession of events, one caused by another, sufficiently explains the cycle of nine or ten years.

Since commercial and financial intercourse has become easier and infinitely more frequent, all civilised countries have been made, so to speak, into

Q

a single market. Nowadays, therefore, a crisis originating in one or two affects more or less all the others. Thus in 1857 the crisis began in the United States in the month of September. By October 13th it had reached its height; discount had reached 50 and 60 per cent., no one could make further payments. All the banks closed their shutters; it was reckoned that there were 5,123 failures with a liability of £60,000,000. In November the crisis reached England, and raged there with unexampled violence. From England it was launched on Hamburg, and the Scandinavian markets, Copenhagen and Stockholm. It then made itself successively felt in North Germany, Vienna, Egypt, the Indies, Java, and, completing its course round the world, Chili, Buenos-Ayres, and Rio Janeiro. The financial cyclone, like the atmospheric, had travelled from west to east, everywhere scattering ruin on its road. These events prove clearly the important truth that, for evil as well as for good, the union of the human race is becoming ever more potently effective.

Slow crises are the results of a scarcity of the instrument of exchange. That which took place from 1873 to 1879 in Europe and the United States presents a type of them. Prices remain low. Profits are little or nothing. Capital accumulates slowly. The spirit of enterprise is not stimulated even by the fall of interest. All economic life seems enfeebled.

§ 4. Causes of Commercial and Monetary Crises.

These crises arise from different causes—the opening of a new market, a low rate of interest inciting to excessive speculation—bad harvest necessitating exceptional importations of food, a sudden change in the lines of commerce, such as occurs at the end of a great war, as witness the years 1815 and 1871. These different causes may be grouped in the following manner.

(1) A very general use of bonds as a circulating agent. Bank notes, bills, cheques, deposits in banks, are all promises or orders to pay in specie, of which, however, there is not nearly enough for the payments that have to be made. Thus the immense superstructure of credit rests on a very narrow basis of cash. Nine-tenths of the business done in England and the United States, and three-fourths of that of the Continent, are regulated by means of credit. The mechanism brought to this perfection works admirably so long as it is supported by confidence, but as soon as credit diminishes all the agents of circulation which rest on trust contract also, and there is a fall of prices. If the contraction and consequent fall are sudden and great, then we have a crisis.

(2) During the period of expansion a large number of debts for short terms are contracted, sometimes in the form of subscriptions to issues of shares and bonds not fully paid up, *i.e.* where the capital has to be paid in successive instalments;

Q 2

sometimes in large purchases of bills and goods on credit in the hope of a rise in prices; sometimes in numerous foreign investments prompted by the low rate of interest, &c. This enormous mass of debts based upon credit constitutes, so to say, the morbid element of the crisis.

(3) The immediate cause of a crisis is always a decrease in the quantity of ready money induced sometimes by exportation, sometimes by the wants of the national commerce. This decrease contracts the resources of the banks which keep the machinery of credit in motion. With this cessation of the ordinary functions of the banks exchanges and payments fall off or cease altogether, and hence arise losses, ruin, bankruptcies, and, in one word, a crisis.

§ 5. Means of preventing and remedying Crises.

To ward off or cure a disease it is necessary to attack its causes. The nature of the causes indicates that of the remedies.

(1) The amount of metal money should be kept sufficiently large to serve as an adequate basis to the credit employed. The best writers agree that England and the United States have failed to maintain this proportion. France has suffered less from crises than these two countries because its circulation of specie is relatively greater. The losses occasioned by crises greatly exceed the saving effected on the reduced use of coin.

(2) In periods of excessive expansion time engagements should be checked rather than multiplied.

(3) The rate of discount should be raised in good time, either to moderate excessive expansion or to recall money that has left the country. A higher rate of discount, by lowering prices, brings back buyers and specie with them.

§ 6. Industrial Crises.

These crises are not general like the preceding ones, but attack sometimes one industry, sometimes another. Several causes produce them.

(1) The closing of an important market, as in 1864, when all the southern ports of the United States were blockaded.

(2) Competition from a fresh quarter, such as the agriculture of Western Europe is suffering at the present time from the supply of corn furnished by the United States at very low prices.

(3) Excess of production. When an industry has yielded exceptional profits a large amount of capital is invested in it, and too many manufactories established. Production surpasses the needs of consumption. Prices fall, and the manufacturers not supplied with the best machinery are ruined. There is a crisis of "over-production."

§ 7. Speculative Crises or Crashes.

Crises of this class have been called "crashes," because their mode of manifestation is by a sudden

collapse. Any one who wishes to learn their nature
and causes should read the history of the "system"
of Law. Law was a Scotchman who arrived in
France in 1715. By his knowledge of finance, and
brilliant genius, he seduced the Regent, who placed
all the power of the state at his disposal. So supported, Law founded a bank on the model of the
Bank of England, created commercial companies like
those of Holland, obtained a monopoly of all the
trade with Asia, Africa, and America, farmed the
taxes, and repaid the national debt of fifteen hundred
million francs. To effect these vast operations he
issued 624,000 shares of 500 livres, which, increasing
in price to 10,000 livres, represented a sum of
6,240,000,000 livres, and 1,700,000,000 more in
bank notes. He thus at one stroke created an
object of speculation, and the means of pushing it
to madness. The shares were fought for. Every one
was anxious to obtain them at any price, for to touch
them brought wealth. Their price rose incessantly,
until on January 5th, 1720, it reached the insensate
sum of 18,000 livres. Stockjobbers realised enormous fortunes in a few days ; all prices rose and
every one was enriched. Soon the reaction set in ;
shares declined. Law tried to stop the fall by buying them in at 9,000 livres by means of an issue of
bank notes. The discredit then extended to these ;
the public would have no more paper of any kind,
but demanded coin. Coin there was none to have,
for it had all been hid. There was a general collapse ;

and the mass of bonds and notes which at one time had represented ten thousand million livres, vanished with the confidence which had brought them into being.

The characteristics of the "crash" may thus be very shortly explained. The infatuation of the public causes a rise of value. If this infatuation is general, the rise is considerable, maintains itself, and yields enormous profits. This attracts buyers, and the greater the number of buyers the greater the gains; the greater the gains the more the buyers. The shower of gold falls on every one; but with the slightest hesitation there begins a headlong fall, and everything collapses. The imposing edifice was but a *fata morgana* created by credit. When the mirage disappears, no real wealth has been destroyed, but enormous amounts have changed hands. Clever men are enriched and their dupes ruined.

CHAPTER VI.

FREE TRADE AND PROTECTION.

§ 1. Free Trade.

A MERCHANT, on being asked by the French statesman, Colbert, what was the best way of favouring commerce, made answer: *Laissez faire; laissez passer,* "Leave it alone;" and this reply of his has become the watchword of the supporters of freedom of trade, or, as it is sometimes called, free exchange. What, in fact, can be more natural than to allow every one to buy and sell where he can do so most advantageously, whether in or out of his own country?

To raise a revenue a state is still justified in imposing custom dues on the importation of certain foreign goods, though the tax is a bad one; but to establish these duties under the pretext of protecting national industries is an iniquitous measure, fatal to the general interest. By forcing consumers to buy from the protected manufacturers at higher prices than they would elsewhere have to pay, the gross injustice is committed of taxing one class for the benefit of another. It is in this that the system of protection consists. If it be said that the object is to favour labour, and consequently labourers, a double error is committed.

Error the First.—The aim of economics is not to increase but to diminish labour. If I can obtain a yard of cloth from a foreigner by means of one day's work, it is contrary to this aim to force me to spend two. This eagerness to increase labour without augmenting production has been well called "Sisyphism," for it chains humanity to efforts that lead to no result, just as Sisyphus was compelled to roll to the summit of a hill a stone that always fell back again. The goal we should pursue is the increase of commodities and diminution of toil.

Error the Second.—No service, but an injury, is done to workmen in thrusting them into manufactories by force of law and in spite of nature. Thus in the case of Italy it is a thousand pities that the custom-house should have snatched workmen and workwomen from their open-air tasks in this lovely country with its genial climate, to chain them in gloomy workshops for twelve or fourteen hours a day to the monotonous movements of machines.

Free trade by applying to whole peoples the principle of the division of labour, assures them all the benefits it can bestow, and thus greatly increases their welfare. If in a family each member is employed at what he can do best, it is clear that the total product, and consequently the individual shares, will be as great as can be attained. On the contrary, if each is forced by legislative restrictions to devote a part of his time to a labour for which he has no aptitude, each and all will be worse off. Apply this principle to nations, and it is plain that when each country devotes its energies to the tasks which its nature most favours, not only will it bring to the international market the maximum of products obtained with the minimum of toil, but the welfare of humanity at large will be increased in proportion to the increase of the productivity of each country's labour.

A man who, in the wish to be self-sufficing, should constrain himself to manufacture everything he needed, food, clothing, furniture, and books, would plainly be extremely foolish, **nor** is a nation that imitates him any wiser.

If the soil of my farm is sandy, and so better suited for rye than for wheat, the least laborious way of obtaining wheat is, not to cultivate it myself, but to ask for it in exchange for my rye of those who have a clay soil. This plain truth demonstrates the absurdity of the system of protection which would oblige me to grow wheat even upon sand.

The upholders of protection make the further objection that foreigners will inundate us with their produce. Such a fear is quite idle, since foreigners will not give us their goods for nothing, **but** will be willing to take ours in payment. Commerce is always an exchange of produce against produce. So much imported, so much exported. If imports exceed exports, all the better ; the foreigner is paying us a tribute, and we shall have more to consume. If exports exceed imports, all the worse, it is now we who are paying a tribute. Here, however, we are touching on the difficult question of the balance of commerce, the discussion of which we defer to a later paragraph.

Protectionists are anxious to sell much and buy little, in order that the foreigner may be forced to pay the excess of his purchases in cash. These aims involve a great contradiction. It is clearly impossible for the different countries in their exchanges with one another always to sell more than they buy.

The principal cause of industrial progress in a country, is, as we have seen, the competition between manufacturers, each of whom strives to improve, and, above all, to cheapen, his fabrics, in order to extend his business. The more widely competition is extended, the greater will be everyone's profit. Do not, therefore, limit it by the frontiers of a state, but extend it from country to country. Monopoly begets sloth, and protection, routine. On the other hand, the manufacturer who is forced to carry everything to perfection in endeavouring to keep his hold of the home market will conquer that of the world.

A railroad uniting two countries facilitates exchanges. Custom dues on foreign goods impede them. Yet the same men at the same time support two policies, the results of which are thus completely diverse. That Frenchmen and Italians after spending nearly two millions sterling in boring a tunnel through the Alps, can place their custom-house officers at each end to destroy in a great measure by the dues they exact the usefulness of this marvel of engineering, is an inexplicable contradiction.

To be consistent, a protectionist should demand the destruction of machines, for machines and free trade have as their common result the diminution of the labour necessary to obtain an object. Thanks to machinery I obtain my coal at less expense; thanks to the stranger I again obtain it cheaper; the result is identically the same. If we exclude the foreigner we should also break our machines; and thus increase in both ways the amount of labour requisite to obtain a given quantity of coal.

Capital turns spontaneously to the most lucrative field of employment. Protection diverts it from these to the less lucrative, compensating it for the difference by a tax levied on consumers, by the amount of which tax production is again diminished.

As their last argument protectionists maintain that for objects of the first necessity, such as corn and iron, a country should be independent of foreigners, lest, in case of war, it should find itself without the means of nourishment or defence. There is no example, however, of a people having lacked necessaries in war time, and to-day there is even less cause for fear than formerly. In the first place railways facilitate revictualling ; in the second, since the Treaty of Paris in 1856 the ships of neutrals may continue to transport the goods of belligerents. The complete blockade of a state is thus more impossible than ever; and it is the height of folly to inflict a permanent and certain harm in order to avoid a distant and more than improbable one.

§ 2. The Balance of Trade.

The balance of trade is the comparison which a country establishes between its exports and imports. When the total of the exports exceeds that of the imports the balance is said to be favourable, for the difference, it used to be thought, must be paid by the foreigner in cash ; in the contrary case it is called unfavourable, since the country has to pay for the excess of imports by means of the precious metals. This method of calculating is now said to be erroneous. I may export forty thousand pounds worth of goods, and the custom-house records their being shipped. The vessel, however, which carries them is lost in a storm, and I have no means of purchasing foreign wares. An excess of exports over imports is recorded of £40,000, and the country is impoverished by exactly this sum. If on the contrary my goods reach their destination and are sold for £60,000, I employ the money in buying other goods, which on their importation will yield a fresh profit. In this case the custom-house records an export of £40,000 and import of £60,000, leaving a balance against my country of £20,000. Yet it is exactly by this sum that it is enriched. These examples, it is added, are borne out by actual facts, since it is in the richest countries that the excess of imports occurs : in England, for instance, to the amount of more than eighty millions, and in France of late years to about half as much. Thus in 1880 England imported to the value of one hundred and forty millions in excess of her exports. Eighty of these are estimated to have proceeded from freight charges, assurances and merchants' profits, and the remaining sixty from the interests on foreign investments.

The ancient doctrine of the balance of trade was, nevertheless not wholly wrong. Men of business still watch with attention, and, at times, anxiety,

the fluctuations of this balance. As a matter of
fact if the customary balance of exports and imports
has been newly disturbed as, for example, when
payment has to be made for grain imported to
supply the deficiencies of a bad harvest, the debts
created by the excess of imports have to be settled
by means of specie. Money, the medium of exchange
and basis of credit, becomes scarcer, and a "tight-
ness" of the market or actual crisis is the result.

§ 3. The Oversight of Free Traders.

The goal at which to aim is the suppression, not
the increase of labour.   Free trade furthers this aim
just as machinery does ; and thus both are plainly
a blessing.   There are men, however, who live solely
by their labour ; and these, if labour is suppressed,
have no alternative to extinction.   Like machinery,
then, free trade may oblige workmen to remove from
one place to another, from the one in which custom
dues furnished them with a barren employment to
the one in which, with diminished effort, they will
obtain far greater results.   It was a displacement
of this character that occurred in France when the
Revolution of 1789 abolished the custom-houses
which separated the ancient provinces.   Abolish those
which still separate the different states, and the same
process may repeat itself.

When such a displacement is accomplished men
will be everywhere better off by reason of the greater
productiveness of their labour, but they will perhaps

be differently distributed, and this cannot be effected
without suffering. The practical conclusion is that
we should create no fresh legal monopolies by means
of which workmen are settled where nature cannot
yield them a large recompense, but that when such
monopolies already exist the tariffs which maintain
them must be reformed with prudence and circum-
spection.

§ 4. The System of Temporary Protection.

This system has never been better expounded than
by the German economist, Friedrich List, the initiator
of the Customs Union (*Zollverein*) out of which has
sprung the political unity of Germany. The final
object, says List, is the establishment of universal
free trade, but in order that this may bring the
maximum of advantage to individual states, and
consequently to the world at large, each people must
make the best use of its natural resources. Now
a country that is exclusively agricultural is necessarily
backward, witness the past history of Poland. Since,
then, although it is undoubtedly bad for privileges to
give rise to artificial industries, many industries well
suited to the nature of a country will never develop
there unless at first protected, the best road to arrive
at free trade and obtain from it the maximum of
advantage lies through a temporary adoption of
protection.

Although both Adam Smith and J. S. Mill have
expressed the same opinion as this of List's, I admit

neither its premises nor its conclusion. An agricultural country is not necessarily backward. If Poland was so in former days, it was because a frivolous aristocracy which had the disposition of the nett revenue employed it for its own amusement, without doing anything to promote the instruction either of its serfs or of itself. In no country has moral and intellectual cultivation, comfort and happiness been so general as they were in New England before protection developed there the great industries. It is a mistaken habit that measures the civilisation of a state by the amount of the products to which its industries give rise. Civilisation has never been more brilliant than at Athens, where literature and art attained the summit of perfection, but where industry remained quite undeveloped.

Temporary protection is no more needed to-day than it was in the times of Adam Smith. New discoveries and processes are immediately known all over the world, and capital and the spirit of enterprise are ceaselessly seeking to cultivate natural resources in whatever country they exist. Temporary protection, moreover, always tends to become permanent, since the interests created by privilege coalesce in opposing all reform.

§ 5. Reciprocity.

The upholders of this system argue, we are anxious for free trade, but for a free trade that shall be reciprocal and not on one side only. If the foreigner opens his frontiers to us we open ours to him ; if he taxes our goods, we tax his. It is the *lex talionis*, the law of tit-for-tat applied to trade, just the same as the case of reprisals in war. In England at present this system is called " fair trade " in opposition to the "free trade " of its adversaries.

These reply to the argument just cited, " Foreigners inflict loss on you by taxing your products on their importation, but by taxing theirs, you inflict on yourselves a second loss, by obliging yourselves to pay more dearly for them. Because he injures you, you impose a fine on yourselves. Impoverished by him, you complete your own ruin."

The system of reciprocity can only be upheld as an instrument of warfare. In this character it forms the basis of all treaties of commerce. By taxing the products of the principal industries of any foreign country I obtain as my allies in his state all those who are engaged in them, since in order to induce me to lower my dues they will insist on counter-concessions being made to me. Reciprocity is thus the necessary introduction to free trade.

§ 6. Commercial Treaties.

Every state determines on a list of duties which must be paid on the importation of different kinds of goods. This list is called the general tariff. It then negotiates commercial treaties with other states, and grants reductions of the duties on certain goods, in exchange for similar reductions for its own products.

R

Each country endeavours to obtain the lowest scale of duties for the industries whose prosperity it most prizes.   England bargains for its cottons and hardware, France for its wines and silks, Belgium for its coal and iron.

Often the states who are parties to the treaty stipulate that each of them shall enjoy the advantage of all reductions subsequently granted to any other country.   This is called " the most favoured nation " clause.

Commercial treaties are useful in assuring to industry what is so essential to it, the fixity of foreign custom dues throughout the period embraced by the treaty.   ·Nowadays commercial treaties are of more importance than political, for it is on commercial treaties that the progress of industry in each country in a great measure depends, and also what is no less important, the development of commercial relations and community of interest between different lands.

BOOK IV.

THE CONSUMPTION OF WEALTH.

CHAPTER I.

ON THE CONSUMPTION OF WEALTH.

§ 1. What is Consumption ?

By the successive labours of the farmer, the miller and the baker, a loaf has been produced. I eat it—matter remains; of this I cannot destroy a particle, but the property it possessed of nourishing me under the form of bread, *i.e.* its utility, has ceased to exist. There has been a consumption of wealth. To consume, then, is to destroy, by using, the utility with which things have been invested by production.

Utility may be destroyed otherwise than in the service of man. A house is burnt down, an object no longer used, owing, as in the case of sedan-chairs and hour-glasses, to a change in the taste or in the manner of living or producing. When this happens, there is a loss or diminution of wealth, but not a consumption of it.

R 2

Some economists have wished to exclude from the sphere of their science everything that concerns consumption, on the ground of its introducing a separate series of phenomena relating to liberty, morals and hygiene. On the other hand, the ancients only approached political economy in considering the problem of the employment of wealth, and in this they were right, since, in the first place, all production is in obedience to the demand of consumption, and, in the second, the chief end of economical science is to make wealth subservient to human development.

The happiness of a people consists in their rational use of all it possesses, and it is precisely this that all the social sciences have in view. The right distribution and employment of wealth are of more importance than its copious production, nor was Xenophon other than just in his aphorism, "No wealth is useful save to him who can put it to a good use."

It is in the regulation of expenses that morality and hygienics impose their commands on political economy. Out of the number of these we may cite the following—All really unproductive consumption should be suppressed, and productive consumption directed according to the rules of science. Consumption should be so regulated as to favour the development of the faculties, moral, intellectual, and physical. Nothing must be granted for superfluities until every necessity has been satisfied. Lastly, nothing must be wasted. It is the habit manifested in picking up a fallen pin, or utilising the blank half sheet of a letter, that leads to fortune. It is economy that has been the basis of the prosperity of Holland amid its marshes and sands. Everywhere the Scotch proverb comes true, that "many a little makes a mickle." Economy is a duty owed to one's own dependants, and to other people as well, for without economy liberality is impossible. While, however, from the smallest income something should be set apart for those who are destitute through no fault of their own, beneficence should ever aim at the encouragement of labour and not of idleness.

No favour should ever be shown to a consumption that bears ill results. "I have been told," says J. B. Say, "that the drunkenness of the people is necessary to make them insensible to their woes : it would be better to diminish their woes than excuse their drunkenness."

Keep a watch on everything; neglect nothing. Remember the Eastern fable, "For want of a nail the horse cast his shoe : for want of the shoe the rider lost his horse, and for want of the horse he was taken and killed." When Garfield was in command of a division he was wont to say, "Keep everything in order; victory may depend on the wheel of a gun-carriage."

§ 2. Different Kinds of Consumption.

Consumption may be divided as follows :

(1) According to the consumers into *private*, that of individuals, and *public*, that of public bodies, such

as the state, a county, a district or a parish
(township).

(2) According to the time of duration into *rapid*
and *slow*. A service rendered, for instance, a lawyer
or doctor's consultation, is consumed in the rendering ;
agricultural products, with the exception of wines
and preserves, at the end of a few days, or, at most a
year : clothes last longer than these, and furniture,
and, above all, buildings, longer still.

Slow consumption is preferable to rapid, as
favouring the accumulation of utilities. When a
bottle of wine has been drunk, after the fleeting
enjoyment nothing is left. The money it cost, if
spent on a good book, will procure lifelong amusement
and instruction to the purchaser and to his children
after him. When everything goes into the mouth,
the result is destitution. On the other hand, a well-
furnished house forms a nest for a happy and
industrious family. In Holland pretty houses to
which nothing is lacking abound everywhere, even in
the country. The thoughtful and prudent Dutchmen
have known how to surround themselves with " home
comforts."

(3) According to its result consumption may be
once more distinguished as *unproductive* and *reproductive.*

The aim of production is the consumption of its
products in the satisfaction of rational wants.
Consumption is thus essential to production and the
final cause of all economic activity. It is necessary,

however, that while consuming I also reproduce, lest I be left in destitution and everything come to a standstill. Thus consumption is bound to be reproductive under penalty of destitution or death.

Consumption is unproductive when the consumer produces nothing. The do-nothing can plainly only live by taxing the fruits of other men's toil. Powder is used in an unjust war. The consumption is unproductive : nay, deadly. Powder is used in a colliery. The consumption is reproductive, for from it issues the coal which sets machines to work.

(4) Once more, we may distinguish between *consumption for enjoyment* and *industrial consumption*. The object of the first is the immediate satisfaction of needs ; that of the second, the manufacture of articles which will be of ulterior service.

All production necessitates consumption. To make a pair of shoes there must be a consumption of leather, thread, nails, tools, and the provision needed to maintain life during the completion of the work. Industrial consumption is only another name for " cost of production."

The " consumption for enjoyment " of the workman and engineer, as that of the magistrate and instructor is also an industrial consumption, since it must be reckoned as the cost of production of the work accomplished or the service rendered. If the wealth produced exceed that which is consumed the country is enriched ; in the contrary case, it is impoverished. Thus the increase of riches depends on the employment of the articles of wealth. Thus, also, a country is enriched the more rapidly the less the amount of its unproductive consumption, and the greater the productiveness of its industrial.

§ 3. Should the Increase of Consumption be Encouraged ?

It is only the increase of reproductive consumption that can be called useful. Yet desire, it may be said, is the mother of necessity ; and we may be told to look at the savage who stagnates in sloth because he has no desires. It is certainly true that to rouse a man from the life of a plant it may be good at the outset to teach him to appreciate the comforts of existence, but the lesson that is soon needed is that he must accumulate capital, produce more wealth, and, above all, put it to a good use.

Modern times, in which civilisation is measured by the subtleties of enjoyment, tend to multiply wants. The ancients, on the contrary, ever preached that desires should be moderated. He who can say like the philosopher of old "*Omnia mecum porto*" is truly free. The man with a thousand wants is a thousand times a slave, and needs other slaves to procure him satisfaction. J. S. Mill has said, "Our utility to others is measured not by what we do, but by what we do not consume ourselves." In truth it is only thus that there is created the capital from which wages are paid, credit draws security, and industry receives its food.

CHAPTER II.

PRIVATE CONSUMPTION.

§ 1. Luxury.

IN the eighteenth century there was much discussion on the subject of luxury. When a financier asserted that it was the support of states, an economist replied, " Yes, as the hangman's rope supports a criminal ; " and the economist was right.

To be an object of luxury a thing must be at once costly and superfluous, *i.e.* it must satisfy a purely artificial want and have cost many days of labour. This sacrifice of the fruit of much labour to an idle enjoyment can never be other than an evil. It must be remembered, however, that what was a luxury yesterday will cease to be one to-morrow. A shirt for the body and a chimney in the house were great luxuries in the middle ages ; to-day they are necessities even for the poorest.

Ancient philosophers and Christian moralists have vied with each other in their condemnation of luxury. Their instinct for the right opened their eyes to the fact which economic science has since fully demonstrated. Luxury is a source of trouble and wickedness to those who indulge in it, and of misery to every one else.

Luxury has its root in three natural inclinations, of which two are vicious, the third almost a virtue. The first of these inclinations is sensuality, which leads us to seek the most exquisite pleasures ; the second, vanity. Of these sensuality owns some limits ; vanity none. " Heliogabalus," says Lampridius, " used to feed the officers of his household on the entrails of barbels, the brains of pheasants and thrushes, partridge eggs, and the heads of parrots." Claudius Æsopus caused dishes to be served of the tongues of birds that had been taught to speak. It was not sensuality, but vanity that recommended these dishes so insensate in their costliness.

The crown of luxury consists in doing violence to nature, and to this effect Seneca says in speaking of Caligula, " *Nihil tam efficere concupiscebat quam quod posse effici negaretur. Hoc est luxuriae propositum gaudere perversis.*" " He desired nothing so much as what seemed impossible, for the main point of luxury is its delight in the perverse."

The savage is full of vanity, and uses tattooing before clothing. When more civilised, men still seek distinction, but seek it by simplicity of attire and brilliancy of genius. On the one hand, luxury nourishes the vanity from which it was born, on the other hand, it gives rise to envy; it is thus a double source of a moral poison, the only antidote to which is a high cultivation of the intelligence and heart.

The third feeling which gives rise to luxury is the

taste for the beautiful and instinct for ornamentation out of which have sprung the fine arts. Happily this instinct is best satisfied not by the richness of materials, but by the perfection of form. A natural flower is a more charming-ornament than an imitation of it in precious stones, however much these may have cost; and a statuette in terra-cotta from Tanagra is a thousand times more delightful than an idol of pure gold encrusted with diamonds. In any case it is by public, as opposed to private, luxury that the taste for beauty and ornament should chiefly be satisfied.

Is it not deplorable that mankind should, almost everywhere, waste so large a portion of its time in manufacturing useless objects, while so many men and women still lack necessaries? If all the forces that at present are thus squandered were but employed to satisfy essential needs, human welfare would indeed be increased!

Luxury has often been defended, not as good in itself but as supporting trade and industry, and supplying workmen with work. This error, though there could be no greater one, has been shared in by men of the highest genius, and even by eminent economists. The prejudice is universal. Thus in *La Fontaine* (liv. viii. 9), the rich man says :—

> "Je ne sais d'homme nécessaire
> Que celui dont le luxe épand beaucoup de bien.
> Nous en usons, Dieu sait ! Notre plaisir occupe
> L'artisan, le vendeur."

" Fashions," says Montesquieu, " are of the greatest importance. In the effort to gain the favour of empty heads, all branches of trade are continually being extended." Emptyheadedness, however, cannot promote prosperity. Rather, J. B. Say is right when he says, " The swift succession of fashions impoverishes the state both by what it does and by what it does not consume."

Voltaire in *Le Mondain* expresses the same idea as Montesquieu :—

> " Sachez surtout que le luxe enrichit
> Un grande état s'il s'en perd un petit.
> Le pauvre y vit des vanités des grands."

M. de Sismondi is still more precise. In his *Nouveaux Principles d'Économie politique* (bk. ii. ch. ii.), he writes, "If the wealthy class suddenly took the resolution to live as the poor does, by its labours, and add the whole of its income to the capital, workmen would be reduced to starvation and despair." This is exactly the vulgar prejudice, which arises from a defective analysis. In the case instanced by Sismondi, the rich are made to add their income to the capital, but they can only do this by transforming this income into machines, or agricultural and industrial improvements, *i.e.* by employing a number of workmen. Fifty pounds squandered on a fashion will maintain fewer workmen than would be needed to clear an estate, inasmuch as manual labour is less highly paid in the country than in the towns.

The creation of capital always involves the

employment of labour, and tends at the same time to increase wages; since fresh capital requires fresh labourers, and the increased demand for these will cause them to be better paid.

To maintain that luxury supports labour is to assert that every destruction of wealth involves an increase of welfare. J. B. Say tells a story of his paying Sunday visits while at college, to an uncle who was both fond of good living, and at the same time a philanthropist. At dessert, after finishing his bottle this uncle used to break the glasses, exclaiming the while, " It's only fair every one should live." Here we have the popular error crystallised ; if the uncle had broken all his crockery and gutted his house, it is to be supposed that he would have fed still more mouths. On this reasoning, Nero burning Rome is a benefactor of the race, and incendiarism a source of wealth !

To set forth the truth : if with the money employed in replacing the broken glasses Say's uncle had planted trees, he would have rewarded the same number of hours of labour. Not only then would he have saved his glasses, but he would also have had trees which when grown, cut down, sawn, and made into furniture would have brought him in an income, supplied others with the means of furnishing their houses, and benefited workmen by an increased demand for their labours.

Historians and moralists agree in the assertion that luxury accompanies the downfall of empires. The explanation of this truth is that luxury is an even greater violation of the social than of the moral order. Inordinate luxury is a result of an excessive inequality, which gives rise to civil dissensions, despotism and the overthrow of states.

Rightly does Voltaire say, " Luxury is the result, not of the rights of property, but of bad laws. It is bad laws which give birth to luxury, it is good laws that can destroy it." This is one of the effects which a system of equal inheritance in time might be expected to bring about.

Montesquieu says, "When wealth is equally divided luxury cannot exist, for this is only supported by the commodities obtained through the labour of others."

"Were there no luxury," says Rousseau, "there would be no poor." A visit to the Alpine cantons of Switzerland, or to the valleys of Norway will show that Montesquieu and Rousseau were in the right.

§ 2. Insurances.

By ingenious applications of the principle of combination, insurances have become the very embodiment of the spirit of thrift and foresight.

If a large number of people pay an annual contribution proportionate to the eventual loss against which they wish to guarantee, a fund can be formed out of which the victims of the misfortune may be indemnified. This fund must be equal to the average of annual losses, increased by the cost of management. Houses are in this way insured against fire, crops against hail, ships and their cargoes against the perils of the sea, travellers against accident, men against death.

A payment of eighteenpence per 100*l.* on the real value of a house will confer a claim to receive this value should the house be burnt. By the annual payment of a certain premium, a man may secure a capital sum to his heirs. The premium depends on the capital contracted for and the chances of the insurer's dying. The younger he is the smaller will be the premium, since there is a higher probability that he will continue to pay it for many years.

Assurances are based on the calculation of probabilities and averages. Their advantages are great. They free the individual from the mishaps of fate. They set his mind at ease for the future. They develop the spirit of thrift and foresight from which they proceed. They furnish a solid basis for real or personal credit, since the insurance policy constitutes security for the loan. They disseminate the habit of co-operation, and favour the re-constitution of capital.

The sick clubs and pension funds of friendly societies are managed on a similar principle. By means of a daily or weekly deduction from the workman's pay or the clerk's salary, a fund is formed out of which compensation is paid in cases of accident and pensions granted in old age.

CHAPTER III.

PUBLIC CONSUMPTION.

§ 1. The Usefulness of Public Consumption.

PUBLIC consumption is the consumption of public bodies, such as the state, the county, or the parish.

Because money is not annihilated by being spent it has been thought that the consumption of public bodies destroys nothing and favours production. This is the same error as that as to the outlay on luxuries: the money continues to circulate, but the goods for which this money has paid have been consumed.

"The King of England," says Voltaire, "has a million a year to spend; this million, as he consumes it, is returned undiminished." Undoubtedly the precious metal is not destroyed, but the commodities purchased by the king have been made away with, and the people are so much the worse off. Instead of maintaining soldiers in barracks, make them board with the inhabitants of the country; the latter will then soon perceive that there is less food for themselves. The taxes they pay to maintain the soldiers represent the provisions which in this case they would consume in their natural forms.

Thus all consumption is a destruction of utilities.

The problem to be solved is whether the utility produced by the action of the state is greater than the utilities destroyed by its agents.

§ 2. Functions of the State.

Bad governments have done mankind so much harm, by war, by organised spoliation, and by excessive and badly-arranged taxes, that economists desire to reduce the action of the state as much as possible. They consider the state as an ulcer which eats into the heart of the people, and would gladly say with La Fontaine, "Our enemy is our master;" or commend, with Proudhon, that negation of all government which is called anarchy (ἀναρχία).

Nevertheless the progress of civilisation has only been made possible by the action of the state. The definition and enforcement of law is the work of the state, and it is the law which, by guaranteeing the fruits of his labour to their creator, gives production an object.

Bacon has said : " *In societate aut vis aut lex valet.*" " the ruling power in society is either force or law." Where it is law, there is order, industry, economy, formation of capital, science, prosperity. Where it is force, there is strife, robbery, indolence, and misery.

The state, by making roads and protecting those who travel by them, has favoured exchange, the division of labour, large manufactures, commerce, the enrichment and unification of the human race. By

s

providing instruction it diffuses science and the indispensable knowledge which together are, as we have seen, the principal sources of prosperity and true civilisation. Lastly, the first interest of a people is that justice should be well organised; in other words, that its administration should be upright, speedy, and inexpensive. Only the state can secure this.

Some years ago a President of New Granada, thoroughly imbued with political economy in all its purity, announced that henceforth the state, restricted to its true functions, would leave everything to individual enterprise. In a short time roads were destroyed, harbours choked with sand, public security utterly lost, and education nowhere to be found. A return had been made to barbarism and the life in the primitive forests.

In Turkey the state does nothing, having no funds at its disposal; it is imprudent, however, to try personally to ascertain the advantages of the system.

All public consumption is so much withdrawn from private consumption; but the first is often much the more useful of the two. Apply the taxes on truffles and wine to public libraries and schools, and no one will have cause for complaint, not even the payers of the taxes.

"Public expenditure," says Rossi, "is a method of making the national co-operation a benefit not only to some, but to all its members."

§ 3. Limits of the Functions of Public Bodies.

On this subject two opposite doctrines are upheld : the doctrine of the state as policeman and the doctrine of the state as providence. In the first the state confines itself to guaranteeing security ; in the second it assures to each of its subjects what is necessary and useful for them. The first doctrine is that of individualism, and maintains that from the perfection of individuals will result that perfection of the state which consists in its self-effacement. The second doctrine is that of the socialism of which Plato's Republic is the model, and maintains that when once the state is made perfect the perfection of its individual members will necessarily follow.

Between these two extreme doctrines Adam Smith has preserved the mean, nor can his definition of the functions of government be improved. According to him the functions of a state are :—

I. "The duty of protecting the society from the violence and invasion of other independent societies." On this point there is a general agreement.

II. "The duty of protecting, as far as possible, every member of the society from the injustice or oppression of every other member of it."

To guarantee to each individual the security of

his person and property, and to support justice with physical force, is an excellent definition of the essential mission of government; but neither Smith nor his successors seem to have suspected its comprehensiveness and difficulty.

To place and maintain every man in the possession of his own is to secure the reign of justice. *Cuique suum*, " to each man his own," is a principle which can only be enforced by the civil laws, institutes, or codes which actually regulate all economic activity.

The third function of the state according to Adam Smith is the task "of erecting and maintaining certain public works and certain public institutions, which it can never be for the interest of any individual, or small number of individuals, to erect and maintain, because the profit could never repay the expense to them, though it may frequently do much more than repay it to a great society." (*Wealth of Nations*, bk. iv. ch. ix. *ad fin.*) Examples of such works and institutions are light-houses, harbours, roads and canals, universities, hospitals, and sometimes schools, &c.

Individual enterprise should be the rule, state interference the exception. To justify the latter, two conditions are necessary: firstly, the matter in hand must be essentially for the public interest; secondly, private individuals must be unable to render the services which this interest requires. Even when thus justified, state interference is always accompanied by inconveniences.

(1) The work it effects is done neither quickly nor cheaply.

(2) Nepotism, favouritism and party exigencies often cause useless works to be undertaken and useful ones to be ill executed.

(3) The action of the state by accustoming individuals to look to it for help paralyses private enterprise.

The historian Bunsen when at Rome saw a house in flames. The crowd was shouting, but no one stirred a hand. Why? *Tocca al governo*—the state should see to it—was the answer he received. In the United States, on the contrary, so soon as a fire breaks out, engines, admirably equipped by private individuals, pour in from every side. Private enterprise is here fostered and on the alert.

Jules Simon remarks, "The state should labour to render itself useless and pave the way for its resignation." He is right, but only on the understanding that the state do not resign too soon.

Under the old *régime* the duties of police were performed in Spain by a private society. This society bore the fine name of the *Santa Hermandad*, or Holy Brotherhood, but it committed the most villainous acts.

If men saw clearly what is their interest, their duty and their privileges, of their own accord they would do everything that was right and nothing that was wrong. All constraint would become unnecessary. The state would be superfluous. There would arrive the reign of that perfect liberty which consists in doing good.

In proportion then to the progress of society the functions of the state will diminish in number and importance. But this very progress is itself, in great part, the work of the state.

The essential and permanent function of the state is the declaration and maintenance of the law. The state is, as Quesnay has well expressed it, "Physical force placed at the disposal of Justice." Its transitory, but no less important, function is to favour the progress of civilisation.

First and above all the state is policeman and judge. But it must also be the road maker and schoolmaster.

§ 4. Public Luxury.

The more democratic a society becomes, the more the state is justified in encouraging the fine arts, the one luxury which it may be permitted. The Athens of Pericles will always be a model for other states to imitate. In his seventh Olympiad Pindar sang, "The day the Rhodians raised an altar to Athene, Zeus brought a yellow cloud into the sky and rained much gold upon the land." The shower of gold which falls upon a people which rightly encourages literature and the fine arts is a shower of pure and unselfish pleasures.

In his *Histoire de Luxe*, M. Baudrillart writes on the subject of public luxury, "At times it invites the masses to enjoy certain pleasures, as public gardens, fountains and theatres; at times it spreads the treasures of the beautiful before the multitudes shut out from the possession of the works of sculpture and painting. There are museums for art, just as there are libraries for science and literature, and, exhibitions for manufactures. In all its forms this collective luxury, if well directed, benefits every one. It raises and stimulates the genius of industry. It has, besides, this supreme merit that it deprives luxury of the selfish and solitary character which it displays in individuals, by bringing within reach of the people the advantages which as a rule are exclusively enjoyed by the rich, or grudgingly shared with a small circle of acquaintances."

Athens raised the level of civilisation by the diligent culture of a love for the fine arts. Artistic decoration and art instruction in schools ought to be a means to the same end. "If education must first deal with realities and forms it uses these as vehicles to attain to the intellectually sublime."

Would not the lower classes on whom material surroundings press so heavily find the best relief to their hard destiny if their eyes were opened to what Leonardo da Vinci calls *La Bellezza del Mondo*, and they, as well as others, were thus prepared to enjoy all the splendours dispersed throughout the world, splendours, which, as Pascal expresses it, when the heart is open to receive them, soften its sorrows and inspire a presentiment and foretaste of happier days."

Public luxury ought never to be supported by taxes on the necessities of life, nor be allowed to encourage among the rich a love of ostentation and sensuality. It should always tend to strengthen those highest sentiments, love of country and humanity, of righteousness and justice.

CHAPTER IV.

TAXATION.

§ 1. What is Taxation?

To defray the expenses of government a revenue is needed.   This revenue may be furnished either from domains or from taxation.

In former times kings derived almost all their revenue from domains, just as a private proprietor now lives from the rents of his estates.   In the present day states still obtain a certain revenue in this way, as in Russia from the crown lands and in Belgium from the state railways.   It is, however, chiefly by taxation that provision is made for the public expenses.

Revenues derived from domains had one advantage in not diminishing the incomes of individuals.   A tax on the other hand, is a fine on the incomes of all who pay it, that is of the taxpayers.   It is the price paid by the citizens for the blessings of social order.   As Montesquieu, well expresses, it, "The revenue of the state is a portion of his wealth sacrificed by each citizen in order to gain security for the rest or the means of enjoying it more agreeably." (*Esprit des Lois*, bk. xiii. ch. i.)

When in exchange for the tax a government gives neither security nor comfort the tax is mere robbery. It is even worse when the robberies of a tyrant help to organise his oppression of his people.

When the tax is moderate, well adjusted and well employed there is no expense more remunerative to the nation at large, or more useful to its neediest members.

§ 2. Rules as to the Imposition of Taxes.

The rules as to the imposition of taxes are of the greatest importance, since national decline and revolution mostly have excessive and ill adjusted taxes as their principal cause.

Even when the expenses of the state are for necessary or highly useful purposes, the taxes from which they are defrayed give rise to much inconvenience. To diminish this inconvenience as much as possible certain rules have been devised which are here given.

(1) The tax should be in proportion to the respective abilities of the taxpayer. Though this principle is strictly just, it was not observed under the old *régime*. Then the rich, in other words the nobles, paid nothing, and the whole burden fell on the poorer classes who alone worked.

(2) The tax should be completely fixed in advance in all its details, amount, method and time of payment. When it is otherwise, every person subject to the tax is in the power of the tax-gatherers. As these become insolent, their victims grow servile ; this may still be seen in eastern countries.

(3) The tax ought not to fall on the means of production but on the net produce. Thus cattle, trees, steam-engines, &c., should be left untaxed. In many villages in Palestine the wealth-bringing palm trees have been torn up, because each tree was taxed. If this tax had been imposed on the land, it would have been the owner's interest to have planted as many trees as possible so as to reduce the amount payable on each of them.

Taxation has often caused more misery by being ill adjusted than by being excessive.

(4) The tax ought to be levied at the time in which the taxpayer will be best able to afford it. For this reason in some countries the land tax may be paid by instalments. So too the succession duties are always readily paid because they are levied from an unexpected increase of the income of those who already had the means of living.

(5) So far as possible the tax ought to bring into the state as much as it costs the citizens. The expenses of collection are paid by the nation and lost to the treasury. Of the dues levied at the gates of French towns twenty or thirty per cent. often serve to support the collectors, who are thus diverted from

productive labour and hamper the circulation of the goods of actual producers.

(6) Taxes should be moderate, and never so high as to discourage production.

"The extortioners of the old *régime*," says J. B. Say, "even used to maintain that the peasant must be poor to prevent his being idle. This theory had as its result the neglect of agriculture, exhaustion of estates, a lazy peasantry, and a misery that often amounted to positive famine."

When taxation absorbs too large a share of the produce, labour is discouraged and economic decline sets in. Under Louis XIV. vines were uprooted to escape the taxes called Aids, which, according to Vauban, often amounted to the price of the vintage. The two most powerful empires of the world, the Roman and that of Charles V., were both ruined by excessive taxation.

In France the taxes collected by the state, the departments and communes exceeded in 1882, £160,000,000, and the net revenue from land was estimated in 1874 at only £158,000,000. The limit which it must be dangerous to pass seems to have been almost reached.

(7) Taxes ought never to be raised from immoral sources, such as lotteries and gambling houses. Again, in fixing the amount to be paid, the taxpayer must never be put on his oath, for this is placing a premium on perjury.

(8) Taxes should not be of such a kind as can be

evaded by cheating the treasury, or an encouragement will be offered to fraud. Custom dues have this effect when they give rise to smuggling.

There can be no worse laws than those which teach law-breaking.

§ 3. Incidence of Taxation.

To fix the "incidence" of a tax is to determine on whom the burden of it shall fall (*incidere*).

The effect of most taxes is transmissible, and their burden is thus divided. The imposition of a tax on the food of workmen will cause wages to rise, since the workman must still live. The rise of wages will increase the price of goods, and thus the weight of the tax will finally fall on the consumer. Raise the price of a shopkeeper's license, he will spread the increase over his bills, and it will be paid by his customers.

After all the changes of incidence, said the *physio-crates*, the whole burden will fall on the land ; no, reply their opponents, it is always the consumers who finally pay it. The truth appears to be that when a tax is of long standing everybody, either directly or indirectly, shares the weight of it. The amount of the several shares it is difficult to state, but the society adjusts itself to the burden, just as foot and boot end by fitting each other.

As a result we may recommend the suppression of as many taxes as possible, beginning with the worst, but readjustments should always be avoided.

§ 4. A Single Tax.

On reading the endless list of taxes invented by
the ingenuity of financiers the question occurs :
Why all these complications ? Why not make a
direct demand on each taxpayer for an amount proportionate to his fortune ? Accordingly various
proposals have been made for a single tax either on
land, or income, or again on capital.

The obstacle to the adoption of this attractive plan
is the difficulty of finding any basis that would
insure the tax being duly proportioned to individual
means. The whole burden ought not to be borne by
land, for land is not the sole source of wealth. Nor
ought it to be imposed only on fixed capital, for those
who draw their incomes from circulating capital or
from their professions—merchants, bankers, lawyers,
doctors, engineers, tradesmen—would pay little or
nothing. Again, to require from every one a contribution in proportion to their income would be the
perfection of justice ; but how is their income to be
ascertained ?

Rather than to commit gross injustices affecting
individuals, it is better to submit to many petty
inequalities of which every one feels a share.

§ 5. Direct and Indirect Taxation.

Direct taxes strike directly at those at whom they
are aimed, for instance, at landed proprietors when
they have to pay a land tax. Indirect taxes are

really paid by consumers, but through the medium of the manufacturers who have to advance them. Thus the brewer pays the tax on beer, but since prices rise to cover this advance, it is the beer consumer who indirectly bears the burden.

Statesmen who maintain large armies prefer indirect taxes, because the people pay them without noticing it. In this way the pigeon may be plucked without crying out. But the inconveniences of these taxes are none the less great : they are obstacles to commerce, as in the case of custom-dues ; they hamper industries, like the sugar tax ; or they diminish the comfort of the working classes, like taxes or salt, beer or wine.

Unfortunately as these taxes are very productive they are difficult to suppress. Two free countries, England and the United States, still derive the chief part of their revenue from indirect taxation.

As a general rule the most necessary articles of consumption, such as salt and bread, should be left untaxed, and heavy imposts should be placed on superfluous or harmful luxuries, such as tobacco and alcohol.

§ 6. The Budget.

The budget—an English word from the old French *bogète*, a small pocket—is the estimate of the state's revenue and expenditure for the coming year.

In free countries the budget is brought forward by the Finance Minister, and passed by a vote of Parliament.

The annual vote on the budget is the weapon by which the legislative power, the Parliament, can impose its will on the executive power, the elected or hereditary sovereign. The holder of the purse strings has always the upper hand. If Parliament refuses to vote supplies the sovereign is reduced to impotence, unless by a violation of the constitution he impose taxes on his own authority.

The budget should be clear, exact, and with securities against a deficit. In modern states this last quality is rare. The *bogète* from being a little purse has become enormous. It grows every year, and is too frequently empty.

§ 7. Loans.

When a deficit occurs in a budget, from some unexpected event such as a war, or dearth, or an excess of ordinary or extraordinary expenditure, states have recourse to borrowing. The budgets of future years are often burdened with the interest and sinking funds for these loans.

Nearly all governments contract loans with a readiness truly deplorable. A statesman who borrows has large means at his disposal. The public who subscribe for the shares find a good investment. The tax payer is blind or indifferent, or, if he calculates, only concerns himself with the facts immediately

before him.   The advantages of the expenditure are
felt at once, the weight of the debt is reserved for
the future.

The greater a government's want of foresight,
the more dangerous does the system of borrowing
become.   In Spain, Mexico, Peru, and Turkey, it has
ruined either the state, or its creditors, and in some
cases both.

The only legitimate excuses for hampering future
generations with a debt, are to save a country,
or to execute works from which posterity will
profit.

The founders of the Republic of the United States
of America could not tolerate a standing debt.
They maintained that each generation ought to pay
its own way.   It is in pursuance of this theory that
the citizens of the United States still continue to
pay war-taxes, to the end that their debt may be
completely wiped off.

The general public so little understands the dis-
astrous effects of loans that it is still ready to repeat
the foolish remark of Voltaire : " A state which is
indebted only to its own citizens is in no way impoverished, and its debts are actually a fresh
encouragement to industry.   (*Observations sur le
Commerce, le Luxe et les Impots.*)

To meet exceptional expenses it is always better
to have recourse to taxation rather than borrowing.
This has always been the theory and the aim of
Mr. Gladstone.   On either plan money, or the goods

which it represents, are withdrawn from private
consumers and employed by the state. The drain
effected by taxation is the more severe, since the
taxpayer receives no bonds in exchange. On the
other hand, the drain caused by loans, though less
severe, is more lasting. Every year the taxpayer
has to sacrifice some enjoyment to pay his share of
the interest of the National Debt. In addition to
this, as Tracy remarks, "The payment of this interest
provides the means of living for a crowd of idle
people who, without it, would be obliged to seek
useful employments either for themselves or their
capital." (*Commentaire sur l'Esprit des Lois*, bk. xxii.)

The national debts of most civilised countries are
enormous, and many states are no longer able to
pay the stipulated interest. The following table
will show the amounts of the debts of the principal
states in 1879 :—

	Millions Sterling.
United States	405·40
Germany	220·00
Austria-Hungary	421·24
France	825·00
Great Britain and Ireland	778·24
Russia	600·00
Italy	408·48
Spain	525·00
Low Countries	82·00
Carried forward	4265·36

T

	Millions Sterling.
Brought forward .	4265·36
Belgium . . .	46·20
Denmark . . .	10·24
Sweden . . .	12·00
Norway . . .	5·24
Portugal . . .	82·48
Greece . . .	20·00
Turkey . . .	250·00
Turkish Tributary States .	21·00
Switzerland . . .	1·40
Total . .	4713·92

Four thousand seven hundred and fourteen millions sterling !

SUPPLEMENTARY CHAPTER.

ECONOMIC QUESTIONS IN THE UNITED STATES.

§ 1. The Tariff and Wages.

THE general question of free trade and protection has been treated in a previous chapter (Book III., Chapter VI.). One argument for protection was not mentioned there, which is much urged by protectionists in the United States—the argument that protection is necessary to maintain the high wages paid in this country. It is said by the advocates of protection that the competition of articles made by ill-paid labourers in Europe would reduce, if free trade were established, the prices of articles made in this country, and that wages must fall correspondingly. Professor Laveleye does not mention this argument, because it is not advanced by protectionists in Europe. On the contrary, in Germany and France high duties are demanded in order to protect the ill-paid labourers of those countries from the competition of the better-paid labourers of England. This fact shows sufficiently that low wages in themselves do not enable a country to compete in another country, and that high wages do not prevent it from competing ; otherwise England could not compete on the continent of Europe. The truth of the matter in this country is, that in those branches of industry to which we can most advantageously direct our labour and capital, the labourers produce a large product, and employers can afford to pay them high wages. If in a given branch of industry, these high wages cannot be afforded, this industry is one which it is not advantageous for our country to undertake. Agricultural labourers in the United States are paid much higher wages than such labourers receive in any European country. Yet nobody believes that the wheat and grain produced by the ill-paid labourers of Europe can be imported hither in competition with our own wheat and grain; everybody knows that, on the contrary, we export these products to Europe. The reason is that the United States have great advantages for raising agricultural products; hence high wages are and can be paid to the labourers producing them. The general high rate of wages with us is due fundamentally to the great general productiveness of labour, which, again, is due in part to the energy and efficiency of our labourers, in part to the extended use of machinery, and in a very large part to our great natural resources. It is in no sense due to the protective policy. If in making particular commodities, for instance, silk goods, such high wages cannot be paid to labourers under a system of free trade, it is a proof that it is not worth while for us to make silks. We can get labourers in Europe to make silks for us at the lower rates of pay which prevail there. We can employ our own labourers, who are now making silks, in producing other commodities—for instance, grain or cotton goods. In producing the grain or cottons our labourers are advantageously employed; and in exchange for these commodities we can get from the foreign labourers more silks than our domestic labourers can produce at home.

§ 2. The Present Phase of the Tariff Question.

Although the protective system directs the industry of the country into unproductive channels, and is not to be defended on economic principles, it does not follow that it should immediately be swept away. A bad state of things may exist, and it may still be difficult to substitute for it a good state of things. It has already been said (see page 95) that the introduction of new machinery, though beneficial and desirable, may temporarily be injurious to those engaged in using the old machines that are to be replaced. A similar injurious effect might result in this country from the sudden introduction of free trade, or even from a sudden great diminution of protection. The transfer of labour and capital from an industry which has been maintained only by the aid of protective duties, to another industry which needs no protection, is like the change from old machines to new and better ones. It increases the productiveness of labour, and decreases the cost of commodities. But it may be for a while harmful to the labour and capital which have been employed in the protected industries. This labour and capital may not be able to withdraw with ease from their existing occupation to the more productive industries which need no protection. The capital can perhaps be withdrawn only by permitting the machines and fixtures gradually to wear out ; the labourers can change but slowly and with more or less difficulty from the one class of industries to the other. Hence any reduction of the protective duties should take place gradually and carefully ; if possible, on a deliberate plan announced in advance, in order to enable the transfer of labour and capital to take place without unnecessary hardship.

It is not likely that a complete abolition of protective duties in this country will take place at any time in the near future. Professor Laveleye has called attention to the familiar fact that direct taxes are much more irksome than indirect taxes. This is doubtless, in principle, an objection against indirect taxes ; because, if the public revenue is raised by the more irksome direct taxes, the people will be more likely to insist on economy in the public expenses. But on the other hand, indirect taxes, being paid in the shape of higher prices of commodities consumed, and not directly out of pocket, are much less objected to by taxpayers. The people, that is, the taxpayers, prefer to pay indirect taxes on commodities, rather than direct taxes on their income or property ; and this may be the case even if they know that the indirect taxes have ulterior harmful effects on industry at large, as in the case of protective duties. In the United States, it would at present be practically impossible to raise the revenue required by the federal government by direct taxes. Duties on imports are the easiest and readiest form of indirect taxation. Being easily levied and collected, and paid almost unconsciously, they will probably continue to exist for a long time, even though the knowledge of their economic badness should become generally diffused. But these duties, if they are to stand, should at least be arranged so as to burden the people as little as possible. They should not be higher than is necessary in order to bring in the revenue which the general government needs. At present the government raises by duties $100,000,000 a year more than it needs. This is indefensible. Moreover, duties should not be confined to articles which are produced in the country, that is, to protected articles. They should be levied equally as much on articles like coffee, tea, and spices, which are not and practically cannot be produced within the country, as on articles like wool, iron, and silks, which the country does produce. The tariff on articles such as wool and iron, which as comparatively "raw" materials enter into the manufacture of many articles of a higher degree of manufacture, is also disadvantageous, in that it increases prices at home, and stands in the way of making sales abroad. In our present tariff, wool, iron, and silks are taxed; while articles like tea and coffee, almost without exception, are admitted duty-free. This is a great mistake. Duties on tea and coffee have no such effect as do those on wool and iron; namely, that of turning the industry of the country into unproductive channels. They act merely as taxes, like the internal taxes on tobacco and spirits, and for this reason are greatly preferable to duties on wool and iron. If any duties are to be removed, the latter should be the first taken off. Even if the revenues must be raised chiefly by duties on imports, these should primarily be levied on articles not produced in the country. The opposite policy, that of levying protective duties on articles like wool and iron, in preference to purely revenue duties on articles like tea and coffee, has been followed in this country; and this is one of the most emphatically bad features of the existing tariff.

§ 3. The Internal Taxes.

The government at present raises a large part of
its revenue by means of internal taxes, chiefly on
spirits and tobacco.   The revenue from these sources
has been, on the average of recent years, about
$120,000,000 yearly, of which more than two-thirds is
derived from spirits and fermented liquors.   It has
been proposed to abolish these taxes, in order that the
duties on imports may be retained without change.
This would be highly impolitic.   Taxes on articles
like these are little regarded by the consumer who
pays them.   If he finds the taxes heavy, he can escape
them by refraining from consuming spirits or tobacco,
or diminish them by consuming less of these articles.
Such a decrease of consumption is not to be regretted,
as it would be in the case of wool, or iron, or sugar ;
for these are mainly taxes on bad habits and vices.
They are, moreover, easily collected and bring in a
large revenue.   As compared with our import duties,
they have the great advantage of not diverting the
industry of the country from productive occupations
to less productive ones.

§ 4. The Money of the United States.

The chief quality necessary for money is stability
in value.   The precious metals have been chosen to
perform the functions of money because they possess
this quality in a preëminent degree.   Paper money
has some advantages over the precious metals, but the
only way in which effectually and certainly to secure
for it the essential quality of stability of value, is to

base it on specie, and to make it immediately and un-
failingly exchangeable for specie.   There is no strong
intrinsic objection against the issue of paper money
by the government.   The objections are of a practical
kind.   A government is likely to overissue its promises to pay, and when it overissues, it cannot be compelled to redeem and contract them, as a bank can be
compelled.   The temptation to governments to overissue is strong.   The printing of paper money is the
easiest of all methods of raising revenue.   Moreover,
there are always many ignorant and unthinking people who believe that abundance of money is in itself
a good thing; and debtors are apt to be in favor of
measures which, by raising prices, make easier the
payment of their debts.   All experience proves that
there is no more baneful expedient than the overissue
of paper money; and, since governments are under
such strong temptations to overissue, it is best that
they should not issue at all.   Banks, which are
compelled to redeem in case of overissue, are more
safely to be entrusted with the issue of notes.   It is
also said, in favor of the issue of notes by banks, that
they accommodate their issues to the demands of trade,
increasing them as more money is wanted, and decreas-
ing them as less money is wanted.   It may be doubted,
however, whether their flexibility exists to a very great
extent; it certainly does not exist, to a sufficient degree to be of great utility, in our national bank system.   But under our national bank system the security for the redemption of the notes is absolute; the
danger of overissue by the banks does not exist.   As
the issue of notes is based on a special deposit of bonds

of the United States at the government treasury, the
objection which Professor Laveleye makes (page 222)
against the issue of notes by banks whose stockholders
have a limited liability for the debts of the banks, does
not apply. When a good system exists, no needless
change should be made from it. The national bank
system should therefore be retained as long as possible. At present the high price of government bonds,
the low rate of interest on them, and the tax on the
notes issued by the banks, make the notes a source of
so little profit that there is a tendency among the
banks to give up their circulation. By abolishing the
tax on circulation, and re-arranging the government
bonds in such a way that their market price may be
nearer their par value (on which latter alone the circulation is based), the circulation may again be made
a source of profit sufficient to induce its retention.

It is not, however, desirable that the national debt
be retained forever. It is being paid off, as it should
be, though at present with needless haste. As the
government bonds are gradually redeemed, the basis
of the national bank-notes will be taken away, and
these notes must be withdrawn. Sooner or later some
substitute for them must be found. To have that
substitute consist entirely of specie would be need-
lessly costly. It has already been said that there are
strong practical objections against the issue of paper
money by the government, but it is possible that the
national bank notes, as they are withdrawn, will be
replaced by government notes, similar to those now in
circulation. If the government, however, is to issue
notes, rigorous measures should be taken that the

issue be limited, and that the notes be made certainly and immediately convertible into specie. The government should under no circumstances issue more notes than there are bank-notes withdrawn; and it should always keep on hand an ample reserve of specie, with which to pay notes presented for redemption. If the specie reserve is to bear a proportion to the note issue, it should be at least one-third of it. The best plan probably would be one similar to that now pursued by the English government in regard to the Bank of England notes. Let a certain amount of notes be issued; let this quantity be decidedly less than the amount of specie which the country would need in the absence of paper money; for every note issued over and above this quantity let the government keep dollar for dollar in specie.

§ 5. The Silver Question.

In the previous section *specie* has been spoken of as the necessary basis for paper money. Should that specie consist of both silver and gold, or only of the latter of these metals? The considerations which bear in favor of the general retention of silver, concurrently with gold, as part of the money of civilized countries, have been stated by Professor Laveleye (pages 202, 203). The most important argument is the greater danger of fluctuations in the value of money, if gold were the only metal freely coined. It is said, for instance, that at the present time, if gold be retained as the standard by civilized nations, there is danger of an appreciation in the value of gold—that is, of a general fall of prices—on account of the comparatively

limited quantity of gold, and the very large and growing quantity of exchanges which that gold must effect.
This danger is probably exaggerated by the opponents
of the gold standard.   It is by no means clear that any
permanent tendency toward a fall of general prices
exists.   The argument at most is good against a
farther extension of the single gold standard, in
countries where that standard does not yet exist ; it
does not bear with force in favor of a change to a
double standard, in countries where a gold standard
now exists.   On the other hand, there are very strong
considerations against the free coinage of silver.   The
simplicity of a single standard is in itself an advantage.
Silver is bulky for any but small transactions.   The
commercial community have a distinct preference for
gold ; and such a preference, if it exist in fact, is a
strong obstacle to the introduction of silver.   Finally,
and most important, it is exceedingly difficult, in fact
impossible, to coin both gold and silver at such relative values that one of them will not be valued differently as a commodity from what it is valued as a coin.
In this case Gresham's law (page 203) comes into operation, and that metal which is given less value as a
coin than it has as a commodity, will be exported.
There will then be nominally a double standard, but
practically only a single standard, for only one of the
metals will remain in circulation, namely, that one to
which the laws of the country give a greater value
than the open market gives it.   For these reasons it
is best to make gold the standard of value, and to use
silver merely as a subsidiary coin.   The difficulty arising from the operation of Gresham's law is recognized

by all rational advocates of the double standard. It is proposed to overcome that difficulty by an international agreement fixing the rate at which the two metals shall be coined by different countries. Such an agreement, if entered into by a sufficient number of important countries, might have an effect in counteracting the operation of Gresham's law. No sensible bimetallist thinks the double standard practicable in the absence of such an agreement.

Whatever be one's opinion on the general question of bimetallism, the present method of coining silver in the United States cannot be defended. The government now coins a silver dollar which contains only as much silver as is worth about 85 cents in gold, at the present market price of silver. This silver dollar is made equal to a gold dollar in effecting payments. If the silver dollar were coined freely, that is, if everybody who had 85 cents worth of silver could go to the mint and have it coined into a dollar, it is clear that silver would rapidly be coined in large quantities. Gresham's law would come into operation. The gold in the country would be rapidly displaced by the silver and exported, and silver would become the specie standard of value. This has not yet happened, because the government does not coin silver freely. It coins only 2,000,000 of the dollars each month. But the fact that silver is coined in this limited way merely makes a difference from the effect of its free coinage, in the length of time it will take for the silver dollars to displace the gold. To the extent that silver is coined, it takes the place of gold. If the coinage of silver is continued at the rate of $24,000,000 a year, gold will gradually be driven out of the country, and the silver dollar will eventually become the sole standard of value. This is equivalent to making 85 cents do what 100 cents formerly did. It is equivalent to reducing all debts, and defrauding creditors, to that extent. It is equivalent to depreciating the money of the country, and has the evil effects of such depreciation. The coinage of the silver dollar on the present system should therefore be stopped. If silver is to be retained as part of the standard of value, the dollar of silver should at the least be made equal to the dollar of gold. To do this in such a manner as in fact to retain both metals in circulation, is hardly possible, as has already been shown. It certainly is not possible without an agreement between the different nations which mean to coin silver freely, as to the rate at which they will coin the silver. Such an agreement is possible, though not probable. The advantages of the double standard to be attained by it, are hardly sufficient to make it much to be desired.

§ 6. American Shipping and the Navigation Laws.

Thirty years ago 75 per cent. of the foreign trade of the United States was carried on in American vessels. At present only about 15 per cent. is so carried. For this great change there are several reasons. (1) Ships can now be built more cheaply in other countries. Timber for wooden ships is absolutely and relatively much dearer in this country than it was a generation ago ; and our protective tariff increases the cost of many materials used in building ships. Moreover, iron steamships have been largely substituted for wooden vessels. The iron steamships can be built most cheaply in England, and can carry at lower rates; the work of carrying goods tends to be given to the iron ships, which can do it at least cost. (2) The war of the rebellion caused many American vessels to be sold or transferred to the flags of other nations, in order that they might escape capture by the Confederate cruisers. By our navigation laws, vessels so sold can never be bought back and again become American vessels. (3) The laws of the United States impose many restrictions and burdens on vessels which are to sail under the American flag. They must be built in this country; they must be owned and officered entirely by American citizens; they must pay a heavy tonnage tax, heavy local taxes, large fees to the consular officers at foreign ports; they must pay three months' extra wages to seamen discharged in foreign ports; they are subject to many dues for pilotage, wharfage, etc. To some of these charges and restrictions foreign vessels are also subject, and in so far they do not, of course, hamper the competition of the American merchant vessels. But most of them affect American vessels alone. In so far as they prevent the people of the United States from engaging in an occupation which they can with advantage carry on, the restrictions are harmful, and should be abolished. There is no reason, for instance, why we should not have free ships; why American citizens should not be allowed to buy vessels built in foreign countries, and sail them under the American flag. If it be said that it is desirable for political reasons, that ships should be built in this country, in order that a naval service may be more readily organized in case of war, the answer is that the present prohibitory system has not caused the construction of ships of the kind that would be needed in case of war. Aside from this, if the government is to be prepared for war, it should make its preparations directly and efficiently, by maintaining an adequate navy.

It has been proposed to pay subsidies to American vessels, in order to enable them to compete with foreign vessels. This proposal should be energetically resisted. It is not in itself a good thing that Americans should sail ships and carry goods ; no more than it would be in itself a good thing for them to engage in growing tea and coffee, or than it is an advantage for every producer to carry his own products to market. The thing to be desired is that goods should be carried cheaply. It is not worth while for the people of this country to undertake the carriage of goods to and from foreign countries, unless they have ability for doing the work as cheaply as foreigners do it. If our industry is not advantageously applied to the shipping trade, let it be confined to other occupations. The restrictions on that trade perhaps prevent American citizens from undertaking the business of carrying goods to and from other countries, when, in the absence of these restrictions, they could do this work as cheaply or more cheaply than foreigners. The restrictions should therefore be removed. But if Americans cannot do this work, under conditions of freedom, as cheaply as foreigners can do it for the country, they should not be paid for doing it.

www.ingramcontent.com/pod-product-compliance
Lightning Source LLC
Chambersburg PA
CBHW031356270326
41929CB00010BA/1211